Twenty-six a

And Other Stories

Maksim Gorky

Alpha Editions

This edition published in 2024

ISBN : 9789362518163

Design and Setting By
Alpha Editions
www.alphaedis.com
Email - info@alphaedis.com

As per information held with us this book is in Public Domain.
This book is a reproduction of an important historical work. Alpha Editions uses the best technology to reproduce historical work in the same manner it was first published to preserve its original nature. Any marks or number seen are left intentionally to preserve its true form.

Contents

PREFACE ....- 1 -
TWENTY-SIX AND ONE ....- 4 -
TCHELKACHE ....- 16 -
MALVA ....- 47 -

PREFACE

MAXIME GORKY

Russian literature, which for half a century has abounded in happy surprises, has again made manifest its wonderful power of innovation. A tramp, Maxime Gorky, lacking in all systematic training, has suddenly forced his way into its sacred domain, and brought thither the fresh spontaneity of his thoughts and character. Nothing as individual or as new has been produced since the first novels of Tolstoy. His work owes nothing to its predecessors; it stands apart and alone. It, therefore, obtains more than an artistic success, it causes a real revolution.

Gorky was born of humble people, at Nizhni-Novgorod, in 1868 or 1869,—he does not know which—and was early left an orphan. He was apprenticed to a shoemaker, but ran away, a sedentary life not being to his taste. He left an engraver's in the same manner, and then went to work with a painter of *ikoni*, or holy pictures. He is next found to be a cook's boy, then an assistant to a gardener. He tried life in these diverse ways, and not one of them pleased him. Until his fifteenth year, he had only had the time to learn to read a little; his grandfather taught him to read a prayer-book in the old Slav dialect. He retained from his first studies only a distaste for anything printed until the time when, cook's boy on board a steam-boat, he was initiated by the chief cook into more attractive reading matter. Gogol, Glebe Ouspenski, Dumas *pere* were revelations to him. His imagination took fire; he was seized with a "fierce desire" for instruction. He set out for Kazan, "as though a poor child could receive instruction gratuitously," but he soon perceived that "it was contrary to custom." Discouraged, he became a baker's boy with the wages of three rubles (about $1.50) a month. In the midst of worse fatigue and ruder privations, he always recalls the bakery of Kazan with peculiar bitterness; later, in his story, "Twenty-Six and One," he utilized this painful remembrance: "There were twenty-six of us—twenty-six living machines, locked up in a damp cellar, where we patted dough from morning till night, making biscuits and cakes. The windows of our cellar looked out into a ditch, which was covered with bricks grown green from dampness, the window frames were obstructed from the outside by a dense iron netting, and the light of the sun could not peep in through the panes, which were covered with flour dust. . . ."

Gorky dreamed of the free air. He abandoned the bakery. Always reading, studying feverishly, drinking with vagrants, expending his strength in every possible manner, he is one day at work in a saw-mill, another, 'longshoreman on the quays. . . . In 1888, seized with despair, he attempted to kill himself.

"I was," said he, "as ill as I could be, and I continued to live to sell apples. . . ." He afterward became a gate-keeper and later retailed *kvass* in the streets. A happy chance brought him to the notice of a lawyer, who interested himself in him, directed his reading and organized his instruction. But his restless disposition drew him back to his wandering life; he traveled over Russia in every direction and tried his hand at every trade, including, henceforth, that of man of letters.

He began by writing a short story, "Makar Tchoudra," which was published by a provincial newspaper. It is a rather interesting work, but its interest lies more, frankly speaking, in what it promises than in what it actually gives. The subject is rather too suggestive of certain pieces of fiction dear to the romantic school.

Gorky's appearance in the world of literature dates from 1893. He had at this time, the acquaintance of the writer Korolenko, and, thanks to him, soon published "Tchelkache," which met with a resounding success. Gorky henceforth rejects all traditional methods, and free and untrammeled devotes himself to frankly and directly interpreting life as he sees it. As he has, so far, lived only in the society of tramps, himself a tramp, and one of the most refractory, it has been reserved for him to write the poem of vagrancy.

His preference is for the short story. In seven years, he has written thirty, contained in three volumes, which in their expressive brevity sometimes recall Maupassant.

The plot is of the simplest. Sometimes, there are only two personages: an old beggar and his grandson, two workmen, a tramp and a Jew, a baker's boy and his assistant, two companions in misery.

The interest of these stories does not lie in the unraveling of an intricate plot. They are rather fragments of life, bits of biography covering some particular period, without reaching the limits of a real drama. And these are no more artificially combined than are the events of real life.

Everything that he relates, Gorky has seen. Every landscape that he describes has been seen by him in the course of his adventurous existence. Each detail of this scenery is fraught for him with some remembrance of distress or suffering. This vagrant life has been his own. These tramps have been his companions, he has loved or hated them. Therefore his work is alive with what he has almost unconsciously put in of himself. At the same time, he knows how to separate himself from his work; the characters introduced live their own lives, independent of his, having their own characters and their own individual way of reacting against the common misery. No writer has to a greater degree the gift of objectivity, while at the same time freely introducing himself into his work.

Therefore, his tramps are strikingly truthful. He does not idealise them; the sympathy that their strength, courage, and independence inspire in him does not blind him. He conceals neither their faults, vices, drunkenness nor boastfulness. He is without indulgence for them, and judges them discriminatingly. He paints reality, but without, for all that, exaggerating ugliness. He does not avoid painful or coarse scenes; but in the most cynical passages he does not revolt because it is felt that he only desires to be truthful, and not to excite the emotions by cheap means. He simply points out that things are as they are, that there is nothing to be done about it, that they depend upon immutable laws. Accordingly all those sad, even horrible spectacles are accepted as life itself. To Gorky, the spectacle presented by these characters is only natural: he has seen them shaken by passion as the waves by the wind, and a smile pass over their souls like the sun piercing the clouds. He is, in the true acceptation of the term, a realist.

The introduction of tramps in literature is the great innovation of Gorky. The Russian writers first interested themselves in the cultivated classes of society; then they went as far as the moujik. The "literature of the moujik," assumed a social importance. It had a political influence and was not foreign to the abolition of serfdom.

In the story "Malva," Gorky offers us two characteristic types of peasants who become tramps by insensible degrees; almost without suspecting it, through the force of circumstances. One of them is Vassili. When he left the village, he fully intended to return. He went away to earn a little money for his wife and children. He found employment in a fishery. Life was easy and joyous. For a while he sent small sums of money home, but gradually the village and the old life faded away and became less and less real. He ceased to think of them. His son Iakov came to seek him and to procure work for himself for a season. He had the true soul of a peasant.

Later he falls, like the others, under the spell of this easy, free life, and one feels that Iakov will never more return to the village.

In Gorky's eyes, his work is tainted by a capital vice. It is unsuited to producing the joy that quickens. Humanity has forgotten joy; what has he done beyond pitying or rallying suffering? . . . These reflections haunt him, and this doubt of his beneficent efficacy imparts extreme sadness to his genius.

IVAN STRANNIK.

TWENTY-SIX AND ONE

BY MAXIME GORKY

There were twenty-six of us—twenty-six living machines, locked up in a damp cellar, where we patted dough from morning till night, making biscuits and cakes. The windows of our cellar looked out into a ditch, which was covered with bricks grown green from dampness, the window frames were obstructed from the outside by a dense iron netting, and the light of the sun could not peep in through the panes, which were covered with flour-dust. Our proprietor stopped up our windows with iron that we might not give his bread to the poor or to those of our companions who, being out of work, were starving; our proprietor called us cheats and gave us for our dinner tainted garbage instead of meat.

It was stifling and narrow in our box of stone under the low, heavy ceiling, covered with smoke-black and spider-webs. It was close and disgusting within the thick walls, which were spattered with stains of mud and mustiness. . . . We rose at five o'clock in the morning, without having had enough sleep, and, dull and indifferent, we seated ourselves by the table at six to make biscuits out of the dough, which had been prepared for us by our companions while we were asleep. And all day long, from morning till ten o'clock at night, some of us sat by the table rolling out the elastic dough with our hands, and shaking ourselves that we might not grow stiff, while the others kneaded the dough with water. And the boiling water in the kettle, where the cracknels were being boiled, was purring sadly and thoughtfully all day long; the baker's shovel was scraping quickly and angrily against the oven, throwing off on the hot bricks the slippery pieces of dough. On one side of the oven, wood was burning from morning till night, and the red reflection of the flame was trembling on the wall of the workshop as though it were silently mocking us. The huge oven looked like the deformed head of a fairy-tale monster. It looked as though it thrust itself out from underneath the floor, opened its wide mouth full of fire, and breathed on us with heat and stared at our endless work through the two black air-holes above the forehead. These two cavities were like eyes—pitiless and impassible eyes of a monster: they stared at us with the same dark gaze, as though they had grown tired of looking at slaves, and expecting nothing human from them, despised them with the cold contempt of wisdom. Day in and day out, amid flour-dust and mud and thick, bad-odored suffocating heat, we rolled out the dough and made biscuits, wetting them with our sweat, and we hated our work with keen hatred; we never ate the biscuit that came out of our hands, preferring black bread to the cracknels. Sitting by a long table, one opposite the other—nine opposite nine—we mechanically moved our hands, and fingers during the long hours, and became so accustomed to our work that we no longer ever followed the motions of our hands. And we had grown so tired of looking at one another that each of us knew all the wrinkles on the faces of the others. We had nothing to talk about, we were used to this and were silent all the time, unless abusing one another—for there is always something for which to abuse a man, especially a companion. But we even abused one another very seldom. Of what can a man be guilty when he is half dead, when he is like a statue, when all his feelings are crushed under the weight of toil? But silence is terrible and painful only to those who have said all and have nothing more to speak of; but to those who never had anything to say—to them silence is simple and easy. . . . Sometimes we sang, and our song began thus: During work some one would suddenly heave a sigh, like that of a tired horse, and would softly start one of those drawling songs, whose touchingly caressing tune always gives ease to the troubled soul of the singer. One of us sang, and at first we listened in silence to his lonely song, which was drowned and deafened underneath the heavy ceiling of the cellar, like the small fire of a wood-pile in the steppe on a damp autumn night, when the gray sky is hanging over the earth like a leaden roof. Then another joined the singer, and now, two voices soar softly and mournfully over the suffocating heat of our narrow ditch. And suddenly a few more voices take up the song—and the song bubbles up like a wave, growing stronger, louder, as though moving asunder the damp, heavy walls of our stony prison.

All the twenty-six sing; loud voices, singing in unison, fill the workshop; the song has no room there; it strikes against the stones of the walls, it moans and weeps and reanimates the heart by a soft tickling pain, irritating old wounds and rousing sorrow.

The singers breathe deeply and heavily; some one unexpectedly leaves off his song and listens for a long time to the singing of his companions, and again his voice joins the general wave. Another mournfully exclaims, Eh! sings, his eyes closed, and it may be that the wide, heavy wave of sound appears to him like a road leading somewhere far away, like a wide road, lighted by the brilliant sun, and he sees himself walking there. . . .

The flame is constantly trembling in the oven, the baker's shovel is scraping against the brick, the water in the kettle is purring, and the reflection of the fire is trembling on the wall, laughing in silence. . . . And we sing away, with some one else's words, our dull sorrow, the heavy grief of living men, robbed of sunshine, the grief of slaves. Thus we lived, twenty-six of us, in the cellar of a big stony house, and it was hard for us to live as though all the three stories of the house had been built upon our shoulders.

But besides the songs, we had one other good thing, something we all loved and which, perhaps, came to us instead of the sun. The second story of our house was occupied by an embroidery shop, and there, among many girl workers, lived the sixteen year old chamber-maid, Tanya. Every morning her little, pink face, with blue, cheerful eyes, leaned against the pane of the little window in our hallway door, and her ringing, kind voice cried to us: "Little prisoners! Give me biscuits!"

We all turned around at this familiar, clear sound and joyously, kind-heartedly looked at the pure maiden face as it smiled to us delightfully. We were accustomed and pleased to see her nose flattened against the window-pane, and the small, white teeth that flashed from under her pink lips, which were open with a smile. We rush to open the door for her, pushing one another; she enters, cheerful and amiable, and holding out her apron. She stands before us, leaning her head somewhat on one side and smiles all the time. A thick, long braid of chestnut hair, falling across her shoulder, lies on her breast. We, dirty, dark, deformed men, look up at her from below—the threshold was four steps higher than the floor—we look at her, lifting our heads upwards, we wish her a good morning. We say to her some particular words, words we use for her alone. Speaking to her our voices are somehow softer, and our jokes lighter. Everything is different for her. The baker takes out a shovelful of the brownest and reddest biscuits and throws them cleverly into Tanya's apron.

"Look out that the boss doesn't see you!" we always warn her. She laughs roguishly and cries to us cheerfully:

"Good-by, little prisoners!" and she disappears quickly, like a little mouse. That's all. But long after her departure we speak pleasantly of her to one another. We say the very same thing we said yesterday and before, because she, as well as we and everything around us, is also the same as yesterday and before. It is very hard and painful for one to live, when nothing changes around him, and if it does not kill his soul for good, the immobility of the surroundings becomes all the more painful the longer he lives. We always spoke of women in such a manner that at times we were disgusted at our own rude and shameless words, and this is quite clear, for the women we had known, perhaps, never deserved any better words. But of Tanya we never spoke ill. Not only did none of us ever dare to touch her with his hand, she never even heard a free jest from us. It may be that this was because she never stayed long with us; she flashed before our eyes like a star coming from the sky and then disappeared, or, perhaps, because she was small and very beautiful, and all that is beautiful commands the respect even of rude people. And then, though our hard labor had turned us into dull oxen, we nevertheless remained human beings, and like all human beings, we could not live without worshipping something. We had nobody better than she, and none, except her, paid any attention to us, the dwellers of the cellar; no one, though tens of people lived in the house. And finally—this is probably the main reason—we all considered her as something of our own, as something that existed only because of our biscuits. We considered it our duty to give her hot biscuits and this became our daily offering to the idol, it became almost a sacred custom which bound us to her the more every day. Aside from the biscuits, we gave Tanya many advices—to dress more warmly, not to run fast on the staircase, nor to carry heavy loads of wood. She listened to our advice with a smile, replied to us with laughter and never obeyed us, but we did not feel offended at this. All we needed was to show that we cared for her. She often turned to us with various requests. She asked us, for instance, to open the heavy cellar door, to chop some wood. We did whatever she wanted us to do with joy, and even with some kind of pride.

But when one of us asked her to mend his only shirt, she declined, with a contemptuous sneer.

We laughed heartily at the queer fellow, and never again asked her for anything. We loved her; all is said in this. A human being always wants to bestow his love upon some one, although he may sometime choke or slander him; he may poison the life of his neighbor with his love, because, loving, he does not respect the beloved. We had to love Tanya, for there was no one else we could love.

At times some one of us would suddenly begin to reason thus:

"And why do we make so much of the girl? What's in her? Eh? We have too much to do with her." We quickly and rudely checked the man who dared to say such words. We had to love something. We found it out and loved it, and the something which the twenty-six of us loved had to be inaccessible to each of us as our sanctity, and any one coming out against us in this matter was our enemy. We loved, perhaps, not what was really good, but then we were twenty-six, and therefore we always wanted the thing dear to us to be sacred in the eyes of others. Our love is not less painful than hatred. And perhaps this is why some haughty people claim that our hatred is more flattering than our love. But why, then, don't they run from us, if that is true?

Aside from the biscuit department our proprietor had also a shop for white bread; it was in the same house, separated from our ditch by a wall; the *bulochniks* (white-bread bakers), there were four of them, kept aloof, considering their work cleaner than ours, and therefore considering themselves better than we were; they never came to our shop, laughed at us whenever they met us in the yard; nor did we go to them. The proprietor had forbidden this for fear lest we might steal loaves of white bread. We did not like the *bulochniks*, because we envied them. Their work was easier than ours, they were better paid, they were given better meals, theirs was a spacious, light workshop, and they were all so clean and healthy—repulsive to us; while we were all yellow, and gray, and sickly. During holidays and whenever they were free from work they put on nice coats and creaking boots; two of them had harmonicas, and they all went to the city park; while we had on dirty rags and burst shoes, and the city police did not admit us into the park—could we love the *bulochniks*?

One day we learned that one of their bakers had taken to drink, that the proprietor had discharged him and hired another one in his place, and that the other one was a soldier, wearing a satin vest and a gold chain to his watch. We were curious to see such a dandy, and in the hope of seeing him we, now and again, one by one, began to run out into the yard.

But he came himself to our workshop. Kicking the door open with his foot, and leaving it open, he stood on the threshold, and smiling, said to us:

"God help you! Hello, fellows!" The cold air, forcing itself in at the door in a thick, smoky cloud, was whirling around his feet; he stood on the threshold, looking down on us from above, and from under his fair, curled moustache, big, yellow teeth were flashing. His waistcoat was blue, embroidered with flowers; it was beaming, and the buttons were of some red stones. And there was a chain too. He was handsome, this soldier, tall, strong, with red cheeks, and his big, light eyes looked good—kind and clear. On his head was a white, stiffly-starched cap, and from under his clean apron peeped out sharp toes of stylish, brightly shining boots.

Our baker respectfully requested him to close the door; he did it without haste, and began to question us about the proprietor. Vieing with one another, we told him that our "boss" was a rogue, a rascal, a villain, a tyrant, everything that could and ought to be said of our proprietor, but which cannot be repeated here. The soldier listened, stirred his moustache and examined us with a soft, light look.

"And are there many girls here?" he asked, suddenly.

Some of us began to laugh respectfully, others made soft grimaces; some one explained to the soldier that there were nine girls.

"Do you take advantage?" . . . asked the soldier, winking his eye.

Again we burst out laughing, not very loud, and with a confused laughter. Many of us wished to appear before the soldier just as clever as he was, but not one was able to do it. Some one confessed, saying in a low voice:

"It is not for us." . . .

"Yes, it is hard for you!" said the soldier with confidence, examining us fixedly. "You haven't the bearing for it . . . the figure—you haven't the appearance, I mean! And a woman likes a good appearance in a man. To her it must be perfect, everything perfect! And then she respects strength. . . . A hand should be like this!" The soldier pulled his right hand out of his pocket.

The shirt sleeve was rolled up to his elbow. He showed his hand to us. . . . It was white, strong, covered with glossy, golden hair.

"A leg, a chest, in everything there must be firmness. And then, again, the man must be dressed according to style. . . . As the beauty of things requires it. I, for instance, am loved by women. I don't call them, I don't lure them, they come to me of themselves." He seated himself on a bag of flour and told us how the women loved him and how he handled them boldly. Then he went away, and when the door closed behind him with a creak, we were silent for a long time, thinking of him and of his stories. And then suddenly we all began to speak, and it became clear at once that he pleased every one of us. Such a kind and plain fellow. He came, sat awhile and talked. Nobody came to us before, nobody ever spoke to us like this; so friendly. . . . And we all spoke of him and of his future successes with the embroidery girls, who either passed us by, closing their lips insultingly, when they met us in the yard, or went straight on as if we had not been in their way at all. And we always admired them, meeting them in the yard, or when they went past our windows—in winter dressed in some particular hats and in fur coats, in summer in hats with flowers, with colored parasols in their hands. But thereafter among ourselves, we spoke of these girls so that had they heard it, they would have gone mad for shame and insult.

"However, see that he doesn't spoil Tanushka, too!" said the baker, suddenly, with anxiety.

We all became silent, dumb-founded by these words. We had somehow forgotten Tanya; it looked as though the soldier's massive, handsome figure prevented us from seeing her. Then began a noisy dispute. Some said that Tanya would not submit herself to this, others argued that she would not hold out against the soldier; still others said that they would break the soldier's bones in case he should annoy Tanya, and finally all decided to look after the soldier and Tanya, and to warn the girl to be on guard against him. . . . This put an end to the dispute.

About a month went by. The soldier baked white bread, walked around with the embroidery girls, came quite often to our workshop, but never told us of his success with the girls; he only twisted his moustache and licked his lips with relish.

Tanya came every morning for the biscuits and, as always, was cheerful, amiable, kind to us. We attempted to start a conversation with her about the soldier, but she called him a "goggle-eyed calf," and other funny names, and this calmed us. We were proud of our little girl, seeing that the embroidery girls were making love to the soldier. Tanya's relation toward him somehow uplifted all of us, and we, as if guided by her relation, began to regard the soldier with contempt. And we began to love Tanya still more, and, meet her in the morning more cheerfully and kind-heartedly.

But one day the soldier came to us a little intoxicated, seated himself and began to laugh, and when we asked him what he was laughing at he explained: "Two had a fight on account of me. . . . Lidka and Grushka. . . . How they disfigured each other! Ha, ha! One grabbed the other by the hair, and knocked her to the ground in the hallway, and sat on her. . . . Ha, ha, ha! They scratched each other's faces. . . . It is laughable! And why cannot women fight honestly? Why do they scratch? Eh?"

He sat on the bench, strong and clean and jovial; talking and laughing all the time. We were silent. Somehow or other he seemed repulsive to us this time.

"How lucky I am with women, Eh? It is very funny! Just a wink and I have them!"

His white hands, covered with glossy hair, were lifted and thrown back to his knees with a loud noise. And he stared at us with such a pleasantly surprised look, as though he really could not understand why he was so lucky in his affairs with women. His stout, red face was radiant with happiness and self-satisfaction, and he kept on licking his lips with relish.

Our baker scraped the shovel firmly and angrily against the hearth of the oven and suddenly said, sarcastically:

"You need no great strength to fell little fir-trees, but try to throw down a pine." . . .

"That is, do you refer to me?" asked the soldier.

"To you. . . ."

"What is it?"

"Nothing. . . . Too late!"

"No, wait! What's the matter? Which pine?"

Our baker did not reply, quickly working with his shovel at the oven. He would throw into the oven the biscuits from the boiling kettle, would take out the ready ones and throw them noisily to the floor, to the boys who put them on bast strings. It looked as though he had forgotten all about the soldier and his conversation with him. But suddenly the soldier became very restless. He rose to his feet and walking up to the oven, risked striking his chest against the handle of the shovel, which was convulsively trembling in the air.

"No, you tell me—who is she? You have insulted me. . . . I? . . . Not a single one can wrench herself from me, never! And you say to me such offensive words." . . . And, indeed, he looked really offended. Evidently there was nothing for which he might respect himself, except for his ability to lead women astray; it may be that aside from this ability there was no life in him, and only this ability permitted him to feel himself a living man.

There are people to whom the best and dearest thing in life is some kind of a disease of either the body or the soul. They make much of it during all their lives and live by it only; suffering from it, they are nourished by it, they always complain of it to others and thus attract the attention of their neighbors. By this they gain people's compassion for themselves, and aside from this they have nothing. Take away this disease from them, cure them, and they are rendered most unfortunate, because they thus lose their sole means of living, they then become empty. Sometimes a man's life is so poor that he is involuntarily compelled to prize his defect and live by it. It may frankly be said that people are often depraved out of mere weariness. The soldier felt insulted, and besetting our baker, roared:

"Tell me—who is it?"

"Shall I tell you?" the baker suddenly turned to him.

"Well?"

"Do you know Tanya?"

"Well?"

"Well, try." . . .

"I?"

"You!"

"Her? That's easy enough!"

"We'll see!"

"You'll see! Ha, ha!"

"She'll. . . ."

"A month's time!"

"What a boaster you are, soldier!"

"Two weeks! I'll show you! Who is it? Tanya! Tfoo!" . . .

"Get away, I say."

"Get away, . . . you're bragging!"

"Two weeks, that's all!"

Suddenly our baker became enraged, and he raised the shovel against the soldier. The soldier stepped back, surprised, kept silent for awhile, and, saying ominously, in a low voice: "Very well, then!" he left us.

During the dispute we were all silent, interested in the result. But when the soldier went out, a loud, animated talk and noise was started among us.

Some one cried to the baker:

"You contrived a bad thing, Pavel!"

"Work!" replied the baker, enraged.

We felt that the soldier was touched to the quick and that a danger was threatening Tanya. We felt this, and at the same time we were seized with a burning, pleasant curiosity—what will happen? Will she resist the soldier? And almost all of us cried out with confidence:

"Tanya? She will resist! You cannot take her with bare hands!"

We were very desirous of testing the strength of our godling; we persistently proved to one another that our godling was a strong godling, and that Tanya would come out the victor in this combat. Then, finally, it appeared to us that we did not provoke the soldier enough, that he might forget about the dispute, and that we ought to irritate his self-love the more. Since that day we began to live a particular, intensely nervous life—a life we had never lived before. We argued with one another all day long, as if we had grown wiser. We spoke more and better. It seemed to us that we were playing a game with the devil, with Tanya as the stake on our side. And when we had learned from the *bulochniks* that the soldier began to court "our Tanya," we felt so dreadfully good and were so absorbed in our curiosity that we did not even notice that the proprietor, availing himself of our excitement, added to our work fourteen *poods* (a *pood* is a weight of forty Russian pounds) of dough a day. We did not even get tired of working. Tanya's name did not leave our lips all day long. And each morning we expected her with especial impatience. Sometimes we imagined that she might come to us—and that she would be no longer the same Tanya, but another one.

However, we told her nothing about the dispute. We asked her no questions and treated her as kindly as before. But something new and foreign to our former feelings for Tanya crept in stealthily into our relation toward her, and this new *something* was keen curiosity, sharp and cold like a steel knife.

"Fellows! Time is up to-day!" said the baker one morning, commencing to work.

We knew this well without his calling our attention to it, but we gave a start, nevertheless.

"Watch her! . . . She'll come soon!" suggested the baker. Some one exclaimed regretfully: "What can we see?"

And again a lively, noisy dispute ensued. To-day we were to learn at last how far pure and inaccessible to filth was the urn wherein we had placed all that was best in us. This morning we felt for the first time that we were really playing a big game, that this test of our godling's purity might destroy our idol. We had been told all these days that the soldier was following Tanya obstinately, but for some reason or other none of us asked how she treated him. And she kept on coming to us regularly every morning for biscuits and was the same as before. This day, too, we soon heard her voice:

"Little prisoners! I've come. . . ."

We hastened to let her in, and when she entered we met her, against our habit, in silence. Staring at her fixedly, we did not know what to say to her, what to ask her; and as we stood before her we formed a dark, silent crowd. She was evidently surprised at our unusual reception, and suddenly we noticed that she turned pale, became restless, began to bustle about and asked in a choking voice:

"Why are you . . . such?"

"And you?" asked the baker sternly, without taking his eyes off the girl.

"What's the matter with me?"

"Nothing. . . ."

"Well, quicker, give me biscuits. . . ."

She had never before hurried us on. . . .

"There's plenty of time!" said the baker, his eyes fixed, on her face.

Then she suddenly turned around and disappeared behind the door.

The baker took up his shovel and said calmly, turning towards the oven:

"It is done, it seems! . . . The soldier! . . . Rascal! . . . Scoundrel!" . . .

Like a herd of sheep, pushing one another, we walked back to the table, seated ourselves in silence and began to work slowly. Soon some one said:

"And perhaps not yet." . . .

"Go on! Talk about it!" cried the baker.

We all knew that he was a clever man, cleverer than any of us, and we understood by his words that he was firmly convinced of the soldier's victory. . . . We were sad and uneasy. At twelve o'clock, during the dinner hour, the soldier came. He was, as usual, clean and smart, and, as usual, looked straight into our eyes. We felt awkward to look at him.

"Well, honorable gentlemen, if you wish, I can show you a soldier's boldness," . . . said he, smiling proudly. "You go out into the hallway and look through the clefts. . . . Understand?"

We went out and, falling on one another, we stuck to the cleft, in the wooden walls of the hallway, leading to the yard. We did not have to wait long. . . . . Soon Tanya passed with a quick pace, skipping over the plashes of melted snow and mud. Her face looked troubled. She disappeared behind the cellar door. Then the soldier went there slowly and whistling. His hands were thrust into his pockets, and his moustache was stirring.

A rain was falling, and we saw the drops fall into plashes, and the plashes were wrinkling under their blows. It was a damp, gray day—a very dreary day. The snow still lay on the roofs, while on the ground, here and there, were dark spots of mud. And the snow on the roofs, too, was covered with a brownish, muddy coating. The rain trickled slowly, producing a mournful sound. We felt cold and disagreeable.

The soldier came first out of the cellar; he crossed the yard slowly, Stirring his moustache, his hands in his pockets—the same as always.

Then Tanya came out. Her eyes . . . her eyes were radiant with joy and happiness, and her lips were smiling. And she walked as though in sleep, staggering, with uncertain steps. We could not stand this calmly. We all rushed toward the door, jumped out into the yard, and began to hiss and bawl at her angrily and wildly. On noticing us she trembled and stopped short as if petrified in the mud under her feet. We surrounded her and malignantly abused her in the most obscene language. We told her shameless things.

We did this not loud but slowly, seeing that she could not get away, that she was surrounded by us and we could mock her as much as we pleased. I don't know why, but we did not beat her. She stood among us, turning her head one way and another, listening to our abuses. And we kept on throwing at her more of the mire and poison of our words.

The color left her face. Her blue eyes, so happy a moment ago, opened wide, her breast breathed heavily and her lips were trembling.

And we, surrounding her, avenged ourselves upon her, for she had robbed us. She had belonged to us, we had spent on her all that was best in us, though that best was the crusts of beggars, but we were twenty-six, while she was one, and therefore there was no suffering painful enough to punish her for her crime! How we abused her! She was silent, looked at us wild-eyed, and trembling in every limb. We were laughing, roaring, growling. Some more people ran up to us. Some one of us pulled Tanya by the sleeve of her waist. . . .

Suddenly her eyes began to flash; slowly she lifted her hands to her head, and, adjusting her hair, said loudly, but calmly, looking straight into our eyes:

"Miserable prisoners!"

And she came directly toward us, she walked, too, as though we were not in front of her, as though we were not in her way. Therefore none of us were in her way, and coming out of our circle, without turning to us, she said aloud, and with indescribable contempt:

"Rascals! . . . Rabble!" . . .

Then she went away.

We remained standing in the centre of the yard, in the mud, under the rain and the gray, sunless sky. . . .

Then we all went back silently to our damp, stony ditch. As before, the sun never peeped in through our windows, and Tanya never came there again! . . . .

TCHELKACHE

The sky is clouded by the dark smoke rising from the harbor. The ardent sun gazes at the green sea through a thin veil. It is unable to see its reflection in the water so agitated is the latter by the oars, the steamer screws and the sharp keels of the Turkish feluccas, or sail boats, that plough the narrow harbor in every direction. The waves imprisoned by stone walls, crushed under the enormous weights that they carry, beat against the sides of the vessels and the quays; beat and murmur, foaming and muddy.

The noise of chains, the rolling of wagons laden with merchandise, the metallic groan of iron falling on the pavements, the creaking of windlasses, the whistling of steamboats, now in piercing shrieks, now in muffled roars, the cries of haulers, sailors and custom-house officers—all these diverse sounds blend in a single tone, that of work, and vibrate and linger in the air as though they feared to rise and disappear. And still the earth continues to give forth new sounds; heavy, rumbling, they set in motion everything about them, or, piercing, rend the hot and smoky air.

Stone, iron, wood, vessels and men, all, breathe forth a furious and passionate hymn to the god of Traffic. But the voices of the men, scarcely distinguishable, appear feeble and ridiculous, as do also the men, in the midst of all this tumult. Covered with grimy rags, bent under their burdens, they move through clouds of dust in the hot and noisy atmosphere, dwarfed to insignificance beside the colossal iron structures, mountains of merchandise, noisy wagons and all the other things that they have themselves created. Their own handiwork has reduced them to subjection and robbed them of their personality.

The giant vessels, at anchor, shriek, or sigh deeply, and in each sound there is, as it were, an ironical contempt for the men who crawl over their decks and fill their sides with the products of a slaved toil. The long files of 'longshoremen are painfully absurd; they carry huge loads of corn on their shoulders and deposit them in the iron holds of the vessels so that they may earn a few pounds of bread to put in their famished stomachs. The men, in rags, covered with perspiration, are stupefied by fatigue, noise and heat; the machines, shining, strong and impassive, made by the hands of these men, are not, however, moved by steam, but by the muscles and blood of their creators—cold and cruel irony!

The noise weighs down, the dust irritates nostrils and eyes; the heat burns the body, the fatigue, everything seems strained to its utmost tension, and ready to break forth in a resounding explosion that will clear the air and bring peace and quiet to the earth again—when the town, sea and sky will be calm and beneficent. But it is only an illusion, preserved by the untiring hope of man and his imperishable and illogical desire for liberty.

Twelve strokes of a bell, sonorous and measured, rang out. When the last one had died away upon the air, the rude tones of labor were already half softened. At the end of a minute, they were transformed into a dull murmur. Then, the voices of men and sea were more distinct. The dinner hour had come.

* * * * *

When the longshoremen, leaving their work, were dispersed in noisy groups over the wharf, buying food from the open-air merchants, and settling themselves on the pavement, in shady corners, to eat, Grichka Tchelkache, an old jail-bird, appeared among them. He was game often hunted by the police, and the entire quay knew him for a hard drinker and a clever, daring thief. He was bare-headed and bare-footed, and wore a worn pair of velvet trousers and a percale blouse torn at the neck, showing his sharp and angular bones covered with brown skin. His touseled black hair, streaked with gray, and his sharp visage, resembling a bird of prey's, all rumpled, indicated that he had just awakened. From his moustache hung a straw, another clung to his unshaved cheek, while behind his ear was a fresh linden leaf. Tall, bony, a little bent, he walked slowly over the stones, and, turning his hooked nose from side to side, cast piercing glances about him, appearing to be seeking someone among the 'longshoremen. His long, thick, brown moustache trembled like a cat's, and his hands, behind his back, rubbed each other, pressing closely together their twisted and knotty fingers. Even here, among hundreds of his own kind, he attracted attention by his resemblance to a sparrow-hawk of the steppes, by his rapacious leanness, his easy stride, outwardly calm but alert and watchful as the flight of the bird that he recalled.

When he reached a group of tatterdemalions, seated in the shade of some baskets of charcoal, a broad-shouldered and stupid looking boy rose to meet him. His face was streaked with red and his neck was scratched; he bore the traces of a recent fight. He walked along beside Tchelkache, and said under his breath:

"The custom-house officers can't find two boxes of goods. They are looking for them. You understand, Grichka?"

"What of it?" asked Tchelkache, measuring him calmly with his eyes.

"What of it? They are looking, that's all."

"Have they inquired for me to help them in their search?"

Tchelkache gazed at the warehouses with a meaning smile.

"Go to the devil!"

The other turned on his heel.

"Hey! Wait!—Who has fixed you up in that fashion? Your face is all bruised—Have you seen Michka around here?"

"I haven't seen him for a long time!" cried the other, rejoining the 'longshoremen.

Tchelkache continued on his way, greeted in a friendly manner by all. But he, usually so ready with merry word or biting jest, was evidently out of sorts today, and answered all questions briefly.

Behind a bale of merchandise appeared a custom-house officer, standing in his dark-green, dusty uniform with military erectness. He barred Tchelkache's way, placing himself before him in an offensive attitude, his left hand on his sword, and reached out his right hand to take Tchelkache by the collar.

"Stop, where are you going?"

Tchelkache fell back a step, looked at the officer and smiled drily.

The red, cunning and good-natured face of the custom-house officer was making an effort to appear terrible; with the result that swollen and purple, with wrinkling eyebrows and bulging eyes, it only succeeded in being funny.

"You've been warned before: don't you dare to come upon the wharf, or I'll break every rib in your body!" fiercely exclaimed the officer.

"How do you do, Semenitch! I haven't seen you for a long time," quietly replied Tchelkache, extending his hand.

"I could get along without ever seeing you! Go about your business!"

However, Semenitch shook the hand that was extended to him.

"You're just the one I want to see," pursued Tchelkache, without loosening the hold of his hooked fingers on Semenitch's hand, and shaking it familiarly. "Have you seen Michka?"

"What Michka? I don't know any Michka! Get along with you, friend, or the inspector'll see you; he—"

"The red-haired fellow who used to work with me on board the 'Kostroma,'" continued Tchelkache, unmoved.

"Who stole with you would be nearer the truth! Your Michka has been sent to the hospital: his leg was crushed under a bar of iron. Go on, friend, take my advice or else I shall have to beat you."

"Ah!—And you were saying: I don't know Michka! You see that you do know him. What's put you out, Semenitch?"

"Enough, Grichka, say no more and off with you—"

The officer was getting angry and, darting apprehensive glances on either side, tried to free his hand from the firm grasp of Tchelkache. The last named looked at him calmly from under his heavy eyebrows, while a slight smile curved his lips, and without releasing his hold of the officer's hand, continued talking.

"Don't hurry me. When I'm through talking to you I'll go. Tell me how you're getting on. Are your wife and children well?"

Accompanying his words with a terrible glance, and showing his teeth in a mocking grin, he added:

"I'm always intending to make you a visit, but I never have the time: I'm always drunk—"

"That'll do, that'll do, drop that—Stop joking, bony devil! If you don't, comrade, I—Or do you really intend to rob houses and streets?"

"Why? There's enough here for both of us. My God, yes!—Semenitch! You've stolen two boxes of goods again?—Look out, Semenitch, be careful! Or you'll be caught one of these days!"

Semenitch trembled with anger at the impudence of Tchelkache; he spat upon the ground in a vain effort to speak. Tchelkache let go his hand and turned back quietly and deliberately at the entrance to the wharf. The officer, swearing like a trooper, followed him.

Tchelkache had recovered his spirits; he whistled softly between his teeth, and, thrusting his hands in his trousers' pockets, walked slowly, like a man who has nothing to do, throwing to the right and left scathing remarks and jests. He received replies in kind.

"Happy Grichka, what good care the authorities take of him!" cried someone in a group of 'longshoremen who had eaten their dinner and were lying, stretched out on the ground.

"I have no shoes; Semenitch is afraid that I may hurt my feet," replied Tchelkache.

They reached the gate. Two soldiers searched Tchelkache and pushed him gently aside.

"Don't let him come back again!" cried Semenitch, who had remained inside.

Tchelkache crossed the road and seated himself on a stepping-block in front of the inn door. From the wharf emerged an interminable stream of loaded wagons. From the opposite direction arrived empty wagons at full speed, the drivers jolting up and down on the seats. The quay emitted a rumbling as of thunder; accompanied by an acrid dust. The ground seemed to shake.

Accustomed to this mad turmoil, stimulated by his scene with Semenitch, Tchelkache felt at peace with all the world. The future promised him substantial gain without great outlay of energy or skill on his part. He was sure that neither the one nor the other would fail him; screwing up his eyes, he thought of the next day's merry-making when, his work accomplished, he should have a roll of bills in his pocket. Then his thoughts reverted to his friend Michka, who would have been of so much use to him that night, if he had not broken his leg. Tchelkache swore inwardly at the thought that for want of Michka he might perhaps fail in his enterprise. What was the night going to be?—He questioned the sky and inspected the street.

Six steps away, was a boy squatting in the road near the sidewalk, his back against a post; he was dressed in blue blouse and trousers, tan shoes, and a russet cap. Near him lay a little bag and a scythe, without a handle, wrapped in hay carefully bound with string. The boy was broad shouldered and fairhaired with a sun-burned and tanned face; his eyes were large and blue and gazed at Tchelkache confidingly and pleasantly.

Tchelkache showed his teeth, stuck out his tongue, and, making a horrible grimace, stared at him persistently.

The boy, surprised, winked, then suddenly burst out laughing and cried:

"O! how funny he is!"

Almost without rising from the ground, he rolled heavily along toward Tchelkache, dragging his bag in the dust and striking the stones with his scythe.

"Eh! say, friend, you've been on a good spree!" said he to Tchelkache, pulling his trousers.

"Just so, little one, just so!" frankly replied Tchelkache. This robust and artless lad pleased him from the first.

"Have you come from the hay-harvest?"

"Yes. I've mowed a verst and earned a kopek! Business is bad! There are so many hands! The starving folks have come—have spoiled the prices. They used to give sixty kopeks at Koubagne. As much as that! And formerly, they say, three, four, even five rubles."

"Formerly!—Formerly, they gave three rubles just for the sight of a real Russian. Ten years ago, I made a business of that. I would go to a village, and I would say: 'I am a Russian!' At the words, everyone came flocking to look at me, feel of me, marvel at me—and I had three rubles in my pocket! In addition, they gave me food and drink and invited me to stay as long as I liked."

The boy's mouth had gradually opened wider and wider, as he listened to Tchelkache, and his round face expressed surprised admiration; then, comprehending that he was being ridiculed by this ragged man, be brought his jaws together suddenly and burst, out laughing. Tchelkache kept a serious face, concealing a smile under his moustache.

"What a funny fellow! . . . You said that as though it was true, and I believed you. But, truly, formerly, yonder. . . ."

"And what did I say? I said that formerly, yonder. . ."

"Get along with you!" said the boy, accompanying his words with a gesture. "Are you a shoemaker? or a tailor? Say?"

"I?" asked Tchelkache; then after a moment's reflection, he added:

"I'm a fisherman."

"A fisherman? Really! What do you catch, fish?"

"Why should I catch fish? Around here the fishermen catch other things besides that. Very often drowned men, old anchors, sunken boats—everything, in fact! There are lines for that. . ."

"Invent, keep on inventing! Perhaps you're one of those fishermen who sing about themselves:

"We are those who throw our nets
Upon dry banks,
Upon barns and stables!"

"Have you ever seen any of that kind?" asked Tchelkache, looking ironically at him, and thinking that this honest boy must be very stupid.

"No, I've never seen any; but I've heard them spoken of."

"Do you like them?"

"Why not? They are fearless and free."

"Do you feel the need of freedom? Do you like freedom?"

"How could I help liking it? One is his own master, goes where he likes, and does what he pleases. If he succeeds in supporting himself and has no weight dragging at his neck, what more can he ask? He can have as good a time as he likes provided he doesn't forget God."

Tchelkache spat contemptuously and interrupted the boy's questions by turning his back to him.

"Look at me, for instance," said the other, with sudden animation. "When my father died, he left little. My mother was old, the land worn out, what could I do? One must live. But how? I don't know. A well-to-do family would take me in as a son-in-law, to be sure! If the daughter only received her share! But no! The devil of a father-in-law never wants to divide the property. So then, I must toil for him . . . a long time . . . years. Do you see how it stands? While if I could put by a hundred and fifty rubles, I should feel independent and be able to talk to the old man. 'Will you give Marfa her share?' No! 'All right! She's not the only girl in the village, thank God.' And so I'd be perfectly free, my own master. Yes!" The lad sighed. "As it is, there's nothing for it but to go into a family. I've thought that if I were to go to Koubagne, I'd easily make two hundred rubles. Then I should have a chance for myself. But no, nothing has come my way, I've failed in everything! So now it's necessary to enter a family, be a slave, because I can't get along with what I have—impossible! Ehe! . . ."

The lad detested the idea of becoming the husband of some rich girl who would remain at home. His face grew dull and sad. He moved restlessly about on the ground; this roused Tchelkache from the reflections in which his speech had plunged him.

Tchelkache felt that he had no more desire to talk, but he nevertheless asked:

"Where are you going, now?"

"Where am I going? Home, of course!"

"Why of course? . . . Perhaps you'd like to go to Turkey."

"To Turkey?" drawled the boy. "Do Christians go there? What do you mean by that?"

"What an imbecile you are!" sighed Tchelkache, and he again turned his back on his interlocutor, thinking this time that he would not vouchsafe him another word. This robust peasant awakened something obscure within him.

A confused feeling was gradually growing up, a kind of vexation was stirring the depths of his being and preventing him from concentrating his thoughts upon what he had to do that night.

The lad whom he had just insulted muttered something under his breath and looked askance at him. His cheeks were comically puffed out, his lips pursed up, and he half closed his eyes in a laughable manner. Evidently he had not expected that his conversation with this moustached person would end so quickly and in a manner so humiliating for him.

Tchelkache paid no more attention to him. Sitting on the block, he whistled absent-mindedly and beat time with his bare and dirty heel.

The boy longed to be revenged.

"Hey! Fisherman! Are you often drunk?" he began; but at the same instant the fisherman turned quickly around and asked:

"Listen, youngster! Do you want to work with me to-night? Eh? Answer quick."

"Work at what?" questioned the boy, distrustfully.

"At what I shall tell you. . . We'll go fishing. You shall row. . ."

"If that's it . . . why not? All right! I know how to work. . . Only suppose anything happens to me with you; you're not reassuring, with your mysterious airs. . ."

Tchelkache felt a burning sensation in his breast and said with concentrated rage:

"Don't talk about what yon can't understand, or else, I'll hit yon on the head so hard that your ideas will soon clear up."

He jumped up, pulling his moustache with his left hand and doubling his right fist all furrowed with knotted veins and hard as iron; his eyes flashed.

The lad was afraid. He glanced quickly around him and, blinking timidly, also jumped up on his feet. They measured each other with their eyes in silence.

"Well?" sternly demanded Tchelkache.

He was boiling over with rage at being insulted by this young boy, whom he had despised even when talking with him, and whom he now began to hate on account of his pure blue eyes, his healthy and sun-burned face and his short, strong arms; because he had, somewhere yonder, a village and a home in that village; because it had been proposed to him to enter as son-in-law in a well-to-do family, and, above all, because this being, who was only a child in comparison with himself, should presume to like liberty, of which he did not know the worth and which was useless to him. It is always disagreeable to see a person whom we consider our inferior like, or dislike, the same things that we do and to be compelled to admit that in that respect they are our equals.

The lad gazed at Tchelkache and felt that he had found his master.

"Why . . ." said he; "I consent. I'm willing. It's work that I'm looking for. It's all the same to me whether I work with you or someone else. I only said that because you don't seem like a man that works . . . you are far too ragged. However, I know very well that that may happen to anyone. Have I never seen a drunkard? Eh! How many I've seen, and much worse than you!"

"Good! Then you consent?" asked Tchelkache, somewhat mollified.

"I, why yes, with pleasure. Name your price."

"My price depends upon the work. It's according to what we do and take. You may perhaps receive five rubles. Do you understand?"

But now that it was a question of money, the peasant wanted a clear understanding and exacted perfect frankness on the part of his master. He again became distrustful and suspicious.

"That's scarcely to my mind, friend. I must have those five rubles in my hand how."

Tchelkache humored him.

"Enough said, wait a little. Let us go to the tavern."

They walked side by side along the street; Tchelkache twisting his moustache with the important air of an employer, the lad submissively, but at the same time filled with distrust and fear.

"What's your name?" asked Tchelkache.

"Gavrilo," replied the lad.

When they had entered the dirty and smoky ale-house Tchelkache went up to the bar and ordered, in the familiar tone of a regular customer, a bottle of brandy, cabbage soup, roast beef and tea, and, after enumerating the order, said briefly: "to be charged!" To which the boy responded by a silent nod. At this, Gavrilo was filled with great respect for his master, who, despite his knavish exterior, was so well known and treated with so much confidence.

"There, let us eat a bite, and talk afterward. Wait for me an instant, I will be back directly."

He went out. Gavrilo looked around him. The ale-house was in a basement; it was damp and dark and reeking with tobacco smoke, tar and a musty odor. In front of Gavrilo, at another table, was a drunken sailor, with a red beard, all covered with charcoal and tar. He was humming, interrupted by frequent hiccoughs, a fragment of a song very much out of tune. He was evidently not a Russian.

Behind him were two ragged women from Moldavia, black-haired and sunburned; they were also grinding out a song.

Further on, other faces started out from the darkness, all dishevelled, half drunk, writhing, restless...

Gavrilo was afraid to remain alone. He longed for his master's return. The divers noises of the ale-house blended in one single note: it seemed like the roaring of some enormous animal with a hundred voices, struggling blindly and furiously in this stone box and finding no issue. Gavrilo felt himself growing heavy and dull as though his body had absorbed intoxication; his head swam and he could not see, in spite of his desire to satisfy his curiosity.

Tchelkache returned; he ate and drank while he talked. At the third glass Gavrilo was drunk. He grew lively; he wanted to say something nice to his host, who, worthy man that he was, was treating him so well, before he had availed himself of his services. But the words, which vaguely mounted to his throat, refused to leave his suddenly thick tongue.

Tchelkache looked at him. He said, smiling sarcastically.

"So you're done for, already! . . . it isn't possible! Just for five small glasses! How will you manage to work?"

"Friend," stammered Gavrilo, "don't be afraid! I will serve you. Ah, how I'll serve you! Let me embrace you, come?"

"That's right, that's right! . . . One more glass?"

Gavrilo drank. Everything swam before his eyes in unequal waves. That was unpleasant and gave him nausea. His face had a stupid expression. In his efforts to speak, he protruded his lips comically and roared. Tchelkache looked at him fixedly as though he was recalling something, then without turning aside his gaze twisted his moustache and smiled, but this time, moodily and viciously.

The ale-house was filled with a drunken uproar. The red-haired sailor was asleep with his elbows on the table.

"Let us get out of here!" said Tchelkache rising.

Gavrilo tried to rise, but not succeeding, uttered a formidable oath and burst out into an idiotic, drunken laugh.

"See how fresh you are!" said Tchelkache, sitting down again. Gavrilo continued to laugh, stupidly contemplating his master. The other looked at him lucidly and penetratingly. He saw before him a man whose life he held in his hands. He knew that he had it in his power to do what he would with him. He could bend him like a piece of cardboard, or help him to develop amid his staid, village environments. Feeling himself the master and lord of another being, he enjoyed this thought and said to himself that this lad should never drink of the cup that destiny had made him, Tchelkache, empty. He at once envied and pitied this young existence, derided it and was moved to compassion at the thought that it might again fall into hands like his own. All these feelings were finally mingled in one—paternal and authoritative. He took Gavrilo by the arm, led and gently pushed him from the public house and deposited him in the shade of a pile of cut wood; he sat down beside him and lighted his pipe. Gavrilo stirred a little, muttered something and went to sleep.

* * * * *

"Well, is it ready?" asked Tchelkache in a low voice to Gavrilo who was looking after the oars.

"In a moment! one of the thole-pins is loose; may I pound it down with an oar?"

"No, no! No noise! Push it down with your hands, it will be firm."

They noiselessly cut loose the boat fastened to the bow of a sailing vessel. There was here a whole fleet of sailing vessels, loaded with oak bark, and Turkish feluccas still half full of palma, sandal-wood and great cypress logs.

The night was dark; the sky was overspread with shreds of heavy clouds, and the sea was calm, black and thick as oil. It exhaled a humid and salt aroma, and softly murmured as it beat against the sides of the vessels and the shore and gently rocked Tchelkache's boat. Far out at sea rose the black forms of ships; their sharp masts, surmounted with colored lanterns, were outlined against the sky. The sea reflected the lights and appeared to be sown with yellow spots, which trembled upon its soft velvety black bosom, rising and falling regularly. The sea was sleeping the healthy sound sleep of the laborer after his day's work.

"We're off!" said Gavrilo, dipping his oars.

"Let us pull!"

Tchelkache, with a strong stroke of the oar, drove the boat into an open space between two fishing-boats; he pulled rapidly over the shining water, which glowed, at the contact of the oars, with a blue phosphorescent fire. A long trail of softly scintillating light followed the boat windingly.

"Well! does your head ache very much?" asked Tchelkache, kindly.

"Horribly! It rings like a clock . . . I'm going to wet it with a little water."

"What good will that do? Wet it rather inside; you'll come to quicker."

Tchelkache handed the bottle to Gavrilo.

"Do you think so? With the blessing of God! . . ." A soft gurgle was heard.

"Eh! you're not sorry to have the chance? Enough!" cried Tchelkache, stopping him.

The boat shot on again, noiselessly; it moved easily between the ships. . . . All at once it cleared itself from the other craft, and the immense shining sea lay before them. It disappeared in the blue distance, where from its waters rose lilac-gray clouds to the sky; these were edged with down, now yellow, again green as the sea, or again slate-colored, casting those gloomy shadows that oppress soul and mind. The clouds slowly crept over one another, sometimes melting in one, sometimes dispersing each other; they mingled their forms and colors, dissolving or reappearing with new contours, majestic and mournful. This slow moving of inanimate masses had something fatal about it. It seemed as though yonder at the confines of the sea, there was an innumerable quantity of them always crawling indifferently over the sky, with the wicked and stupid intention of never allowing it to illumine the sleeping sea with the million golden eyes of its many-colored stars, which awaken the noble desires of beings in adoration before their holy and pure light.

"Isn't the sea beautiful?" asked Tchelkache.

"Not bad! Only one is afraid on it," replied Gavrilo, rowing evenly and strongly. The sea could scarcely be heard; it dripped from the long oars and still shone with its warm, blue phosphorescent lights.

"Afraid? Simpleton!" growled Tchelkache.

He, the cynical robber, loved the sea. His ardent temperament, greedy for impressions, never tired of contemplating its infinite, free and powerful immensity. It offended him to receive such a reply to his question concerning the beauty of the sea that he loved. Seated at the tiller, he cleaved the water with his oar and gazed tranquilly before him, filled with the desire to thus continue rowing forever over this velvet plain.

On the sea, warm and generous impulses rose within him, filled his soul and in a measure purified it of the defilements of life. He enjoyed this effect and liked to feel himself better, out here, amid the waves and air where the thoughts and occupations of life lose their interest and life itself sinks into insignificance. In the night, the sound of its soft breathing is wafted over the slumbering sea, and this infinite murmur fills the soul with peace, checks all unworthy impulses and brings forth mighty dreams.

"The nets, where are they, eh?" suddenly asked Gavrilo, inspecting the boat.

Tchelkache shuddered.

"There's the net, at the rudder."

"What kind of a net's that?" asked Gavrilo, suspiciously.

"A sweep-net..."

But Tchelkache was ashamed to lie to this child to conceal his real purpose; he also regretted the thoughts and feelings that the lad had put to flight by his question. He became angry. He felt the sharp burning sensation that he knew so well, in his breast; his throat contracted. He said harshly to Gavrilo:

"You're there; well, remain there! Don't meddle with what doesn't concern you. You've been brought to row, now row. And if you let your tongue wag, no good will come of it. Do you understand?"

For one minute, the boat wavered and stopped. The oars stood still in the foaming water around them, and Gavrilo moved uneasily on his seat.

"Row!"

A fierce oath broke the stillness. Gavrilo bent to the oars. The boat, as though frightened, leaped ahead rapidly and nervously, noisily cutting the water.

"Better than that!"

Tchelkache had risen from the helm and, without letting go his oar, he fixed his cold eyes upon the pale face and trembling lips of Gavrilo. Sinuous and bending forward, he resembled a cat ready to jump. A furious grinding of teeth and rattling of bones could be heard.

"Who goes there?"

This imperious demand resounded over the sea.

"The devil! Row, row! No noise! I'll kill you, dog. Row, can't you! One, two! Dare to cry out! I'll tear you from limb to limb!..." hissed Tchelkache.

"Oh, Holy Virgin," murmured Gavrilo, trembling and exhausted.

The boat turned, obedient to his touch; he pulled toward the harbor where the many-colored lanterns were grouped together and the tall masts were outlined against the sky.

"Hey! Who calls?" was again asked. This time the voice was further away; Tchelkache felt relieved.

"It's you, yourself, friend, who calls!" said he, in the direction of the voice. Then, he turned to Gavrilo, who continued to murmur a prayer. "Yes, brother, you're in luck. If those devils had pursued us, it would have been the end of you. Do you hear? I'd have soon sent you to the fishes."

Now that Tchelkache again spoke quietly and even good-naturedly, Gavrilo, still trembling with fear, begged him:

"Listen, let me go! In the name of Christ, let me go. Set me down somewhere. Oh dear! oh, dear! I'm lost! For God's sake, let me go. What do you want of me? I can't do this, I've never done anything like it. It's the first time, Lord! I'm lost! How did you manage, comrade, to get around me like this? Say? It's a sin, you make me lose my soul! . . . Ah! what a piece of business!"

"What business?" sternly questioned Tchelkache. "Speak, what business do you mean?"

The lad's terror amused him; he also enjoyed the sensation of being able to provoke such fear.

"Dark transactions, brother. . . Let me go, for the love of Heaven. What am I to you? Friend . . ."

"Be quiet! If I hadn't needed you, I shouldn't have brought you! Do you understand? Eh! Well, be quiet!"

"Oh, Lord!" sobbed Gavrilo.

"Enough!"

Gavrilo could no longer control himself and his breath came in broken and painful gasps; he wept and moved restlessly about on his seat, but rowed hard, in despair. The boat sped ahead like an arrow. Again the black hulls of the ships arose before them, and the boat, turning like a top in the narrow channels that separated them, was soon lost among them.

"Hey! You, listen: If anyone speaks to us, keep still, if you value your skin. Do you understand?"

"Alas!" hopelessly sighed Gavrilo, in response to this stern command, and he added: "It was my lot to be lost!"

"Stop howling!" whispered Tchelkache.

These words completely robbed Gavrilo of all understanding and he remained crushed under the chill presentiment of some misfortune. He mechanically dipped his oars and sending them back and forth through the water in an even and steady stroke did not lift his eyes again.

The slumbering murmur of the waves was gloomy and fearsome. Here is the harbor. . . From behind its stone wall, comes the sound of human voices, the plashing of water, singing and shrill whistling."

"Stop!" whispered Tchelkache.

"Drop the oars! Lean your hands against the wall! Softly, devil!"

Gavrilo caught hold of the slippery stone and guided the boat along the wall. He advanced noiselessly, just grazing the slimy moss of the stone.

"Stop, give me the oars! Give them here! And your passport, where have you put it? In your bag! Give me the bag! Quicker! . . . That, my friend, is so that you'll not run away. . . Now I hold you. Without oars you could have made off just the same, but, without a passport you'll not dare. Wait! And remember that if you so much as breathe a word I'll catch you, even though at the bottom of the sea."

Suddenly, catching hold of something, Tchelkache rose in the air; he disappeared over the wall.

Gavrilo shuddered. . . It had been so quickly done! He felt that the cursed weight and fear that he experienced in the presence of this moustached and lean bandit had, as it were, slipped off and rolled away from him. Could he escape, now? Breathing freely, he looked around him. On the left rose a black hull without masts, like an immense empty, deserted coffin. The waves beating against its sides awakened heavy echoes therein, resembling long-drawn sighs. On the right, stretched the damp wall of the quay, like a cold heavy serpent. Behind were visible black skeletons, and in front, in the space between the wall and the coffin, was the sea, silent and deserted, with black clouds hanging over it. These clouds were slowly advancing, their enormous, heavy masses, terrifying in the darkness, ready to crush man with their weight. All was cold, black and of evil omen. Gavrilo was afraid. This fear was greater than that imposed on him by Tchelkache; it clasped Gavrilo's breast in a tight embrace, squeezed him to a helpless mass and riveted him to the boat's bench.

Perfect silence reigned. Not a sound, save the sighs of the seas; it seemed as though this silence was about to be suddenly broken by some frightful, furious explosion of sound that would shake the sea to its depths, tear apart the dark masses of clouds floating over the sky and bury under the waves all those black craft. The clouds crawled over the sky as slowly and as wearily as before, but the sea gradually emerged from under them, and one might fancy, looking at the sky, that it was also a sea, but an angry sea overhanging a peaceful, sleeping one. The clouds resembled waves whose gray crests touched the earth; they resembled abysses hollowed by the wind between the waves and nascent billows not yet covered with the green foam of fury.

Gavrilo was oppressed by this dark calm and beauty; he realized that he desired his master's return. But he did not come! The time passed slowly, more slowly than crawled the clouds up in the sky. . . And the length of time augmented the agony of the silence. But just now behind the wall, the plashing of water was heard, then a rustling, and something like a whisper. Gavrilo was half dead from fright.

"Hey, there! Are you asleep? Take this! Softly!" said Tchelkache's hoarse voice.

From the wall descended a solid, square, heavy object. Gavrilo put it in the boat, then another one like it. Across the wall stretched Tchelkache's long figure. The oars reappeared mysteriously, then Gavrilo's bag fell at his feet and Tchelkache out of breath seated himself at the tiller.

Gavrilo looked at him with a timid and glad smile.

"Are you tired?" said he.

"A little, naturally, simpleton! Row firm, with all your might. You have a pretty profit, brother! The affair is half done, now there only remains to pass unseen under the eyes of those devils, and then you'll receive your money and fly to your Machka... You have a Machka, say, little one?"

"N-no!"

Gavrilo did not spare himself; his breast worked like a bellows and his arms like steel springs. The water foamed under the boat and the blue trail that followed in the wake of the stern had become wider. Gavrilo was bathed in perspiration, but he continued to row with all his strength. After twice experiencing the fright that he had on this night, he dreaded a repetition of it and had only one desire: to finish this accursed task as soon as possible, regain the land, and flee from this man before he should be killed by him or imprisoned on account of his misdeeds. He resolved not to speak to him, not to contradict him in anything, to execute all his commands and if he succeeded in freeing himself from him unmolested, to sing a Te Deum to Saint Nicholas. An earnest prayer was on his lips. But he controlled himself, puffed like a steamboat, and in silence cast furtive glances at Tchelkache.

The other, bending his long, lean body forward, like a bird poising for flight, gazed ahead into the darkness with his hawk's eyes. Turning his fierce, aquiline nose from side to side, he held the tiller with one hand and with the other tugged at his moustache which by a constant trembling betrayed the quiet smile on the thin lips. Tchelkache was pleased with his success, with himself and with this lad, whom he had terrified into becoming his slave. He enjoyed in advance to-morrow's feast and now he rejoiced in his strength and the subjection of this young, untried boy. He saw him toil; he took pity on him and tried to encourage him.

"Hey! Say there!" he asked softly. "Were you very much afraid?"

"It doesn't matter!" sighed Gavrilo, coughing.

"You needn't keep on rowing so hard. It's ended, now. There's only one more bad place to pass... Rest yourself."

Gavrilo stopped docilely, wiped the perspiration from his face with the sleeve of his blouse and again dipped the oars in the water.

"That's right, row more gently. So that the water tells no tales. There's a channel to cross. Softly, softly. Here, brother, are serious people. They are quite capable of amusing themselves with a gun, They could raise a fine lump on your forehead before you'd have time to cry out."

The boat glided over the water almost without sound. Blue drops fell from the oars and when they touched the sea there flamed up for an instant a little blue spot. The night was growing darker and more silent. The sky no longer resembled a rough sea; the clouds extended over its surface, forming a thick, even curtain, hanging motionless above the ocean. The sea was calmer and blacker, its warm and salty odor was stronger and it did not appear as vast as before.

"Oh! if it would only rain!" murmured Tchelkache; "we would be hidden by a curtain."

On the right and left of the boat, the motionless, melancholy, black hulls of ships emerged from the equally black water. A light moved to and fro on one; someone was walking with a lantern. The sea, caressing their sides, seemed to dully implore them while they responded by a cold, rumbling echo, as though they were disputing and refusing to yield.

"The custom-house," whispered Tchelkache.

From the moment that he had ordered Gavrilo to row slowly, the lad had again experienced a feeling of feverish expectation. He leaned forward, toward the darkness and it seemed to him that he was growing larger; his bones and veins stretched painfully; his head, filled with one thought, ached; the skin on his back shivered and in his legs were pricking sensations as though small sharp, cold needles were being thrust into them. His eyes smarted from having gazed too long into the darkness out of which he expected to see someone rise up and cry out: "Stop thieves!"

When Tchelkache murmured: "the custom-house!" Gavrilo started: he was consumed by a sharp, burning thought; his nerves were wrought up to the highest pitch; he wanted to cry out, to call for help, he had already opened his mouth and straightened himself up on the seat. He thrust forward his chest, drew a long breath, and again opened his mouth; but suddenly, overcome by sharp fear, he closed his eyes and fell from his seat.

Ahead of the boat, far off on the horizon, an immense, flaming blue sword sprang up from the black water. It rose, cleaved the darkness; its blade flashed across the clouds and illumined the surface of the sea with a broad blue hand. In this luminous ray stood out the black, silent ships, hitherto invisible. It seemed as though they had been waiting at the bottom of the sea, whither they had been dragged by an irresistible tempest, and that now they arose in obedience to the sword of fire to which the sea had given birth. They had ascended to contemplate the sky and all that was above the water. The rigging clinging to the mast seemed like seaweed that had left the water with these black giants, covering them with their meshes. Then the wonderful blue sword again arose in the air, cleaved the night and descended in a different place. Again, on the spot where it rested, appeared the skeletons of ships until then invisible.

Tchelkache's boat stopped and rocked on the water as though hesitating. Gavrilo lay flat on the bottom of the boat, covering his face with his hands, and Tchelkache prodded him with his oar, hissing furiously, but quite low.

"Idiot, that's the custom-house cruiser. The electric lantern! Get up, row with all your might! They'll throw the light upon us! You'll ruin us, devil, both of us!"

When the sharp edge of the oar had been brought down once more, harder this time, on Gavrilo's back, he arose and, not daring to open his eyes, resumed his seat and feeling for the oars, sent the boat ahead.

"Softly, or I'll kill you! Softly! Imbecile, may the devil take you! What are you afraid of? Say? A lantern and a mirror. That's all! Softly with those oars, miserable wretch! They incline the mirror at will and light the sea to find out if any folks like us are roving over it. They're on the watch for smugglers. We're out of reach; they're too far away, now. Don't be afraid, boy, we're safe! Now, we..."

Tchelkache looked around him triumphantly.

"Yes, we're safe. Out! You were in luck, you worthless stick!"

Gavrilo rowed in silence; breathing heavily, he cast sidelong glances at the spot where still rose and fell the sword of fire. He could not believe that it was only, as Tchelkache said, a lantern with a reflector. The cold, blue light, cutting the darkness, awoke silver reflections upon the sea; there seemed something mysterious about it, and Gavrilo again felt his faculties benumbed with fear. The presentiment of some misfortune oppressed him a second time. He rowed like a machine, bent his shoulders as though expecting a blow to descend and felt himself void of every desire, and without soul. The emotions of that night had consumed all that was human in him.

Tchelkache was more triumphant than ever: his success was complete! His nerves, accustomed to shocks, were already calmed. His lips trembled and his eyes shone with an eager light. He felt strong and well, whistled softly, inhaled long breaths of the salt sea air, glanced about from right to left and smiled good-naturedly when his eyes fell upon Gavrilo.

A light breeze set a thousand little waves to dancing. The clouds became thinner and more transparent although still covering the sky. The wind swept lightly and freely over the entire surface of the sea, but the clouds remained motionless, and seemed to be plunged in a dull, gray reverie.

"Come, brother, wake up, it's time! Your soul seems to have been shaken out of your skin; there's nothing left but a bag of bones. My dear fellow! We have hold of the good end, eh?"

Gavrilo was glad to hear a human voice, even though it was that of Tchelkache.

"I know it," said he, very low.

"That's right, little man! Take the tiller, I'll row; You're tired, aren't you?"

Gavrilo mechanically changed places, and when Tchelkache saw that he staggered, he pitied him more still and patted him on the shoulder,

"Don't be afraid! You've made a good thing out of it. I'll pay you well. Would you like to have twenty-five rubles, eh?"

"I—I don't need anything. All I ask is to reach land!"

Tchelkache removed his hand, spat and began to row; his long arms sent the oars far back of him.

The sea had awakened. It sported with its tiny waves, brought them forth, adorned them with a fringe of foam, tumbled them over each other and broke them into spray. The foam as it melted sighed and the air was filled with harmonious sounds and the plashing of water. The darkness seemed to be alive.

"Well! tell me . . ." began Tchelkache. "You'll return to the village, you'll marry, you'll set to work to plough and sow, your wife'll present you with many children, you'll not have enough bread and you'll just manage to keep soul and body together all your life! So . . . is it such a pleasant prospect?"

"What pleasure can there be in that?" timidly and shudderingly replied Gavrilo. "What can one do?"

Here and there, the clouds were rent by the wind and, through the spaces, the cold sky studded with a few stars looked down. Reflected by the joyous sea, these stars leaped upon the waves, now disappearing, now shining brightly.

"More to the left!" said Tchelkache. "We shall soon be there, Yes! . . . it is ended. We've done a good stroke of work. In a single night, you understand—five hundred rubles gained! Isn't that doing well, say?"

"Five hundred rubles!" repeated Gavrilo, distrustfully, but he was immediately seized with fright and quickly asked, kicking the bales at the bottom of the boat: "What are those things?"

"That's silk. A very dear thing. If it were to be sold for its real value, it would bring a thousand rubles. But I don't raise the price . . . clever that, eh?"

"Is it possible?" asked Gavrilo. "If I only had as much!"

He sighed at the thought of the country, of his miserable life, his toil, his mother and all those far-distant and dear things for which he had gone away to work, and for which he had suffered so much that night. A wave of memory swept over him: he saw his village on a hill-side with the river at the bottom, hidden by birches, willows, mountain-ash and wild cherry trees. The picture breathed some life in him and gave him a little strength.

"Oh, Lord, how much good it would do!" he sighed, sadly.

"Yes! I imagine that you'd very quickly board the train and—good-evening! Oh, how the girls would love you, yonder, in the village! You could have your pick. You could have a new house built. But for a new house, there might not be enough . . ."

"That's true. A house, no; wood is very dear with us."

"Never mind, you could have the one that you have repaired. Do you own a horse?"

"A horse? Yes, there's one, but he's very old!"

"Then a horse, a good horse! A cow . . . sheep . . . poultry . . . eh?"

"Why do you say that? If only! . . . Ah! Lord, how I might enjoy life."

"Yes, brother, life under those circumstances would not be bad . . . I, too, I know a little about such things. I also have a nest belonging to me. My father was one of the richest peasants of his village."

Tchelkache rowed slowly. The boat danced upon the waves which beat against its sides; it scarcely advanced over the somber sea, now disporting itself harder than ever. The two men dreamed, rocked upon the water and gazing vaguely around them. Tchelkache had spoken to Gavrilo of his village with the purpose of quieting him and helping him to recover from his emotion. He at first spoke with a sceptical smile hidden under his moustache, but as he talked and recalled the joys of country life, in regard to which he himself had long since been disabused, and that he had forgotten until this moment, he became carried away, and instead of talking to the lad, he began unconsciously to harangue:

"The essential part of the life of a peasant, brother, is liberty. You must be your own master. You own your house: it is not worth much, but it belongs to you. You possess a piece of ground, a little corner, perhaps, but it is yours. Your chickens, eggs, apples are yours. You are a king upon the earth. Then you must be methodical... As soon as you are up in the morning, you must go to work. In the spring it is one thing, in the summer another, in the autumn and winter still another. From wherever you may be you always return to your home. There is warmth, rest!... You are a king, are you not?"

Tchelkache had waxed enthusiastic over this long enumeration of the privileges and rights of the peasant, forgetting only to speak of his duties.

Gavrilo looked at him with curiosity, and was also aroused to enthusiasm. He had already had time in the course of this conversation to forget with whom he was dealing; he saw before him only a peasant like himself, attached to the earth by labor, by several generations of laborers, by memories of childhood, but who had voluntarily withdrawn from it and its cares and who was now suffering the punishment of his ill-advised act.

"Yes, comrade, that's true! Oh! how true that is! See now, take your case, for instance: what are you now, without land? Ah! friend, the earth is like a mother: one doesn't forget it long."

Tchelkache came to himself. He felt within him that burning sensation that always seized upon him when his self-love as a dashing devil-may-care fellow was wounded, especially when the offender was of no account in his eyes.

"There he goes again!" he exclaimed fiercely. "You imagine, I suppose that I'm speaking seriously. I'm worth more than that, let me tell you!"

"Why, you funny fellow!" replied Gavrilo, again intimidated, "am I speaking of you? There are a great many like you! My God, how many unfortunate persons, vagabonds there are on the earth!"

"Take the oars again, dolt!" commanded Tchelkache shortly, restraining himself from pouring forth a string of fierce oaths that rose in his throat.

They again changed places. Tchelkache, while clambering over the bales to return to the helm, experienced a sharp desire to give Gavrilo a good blow that would send him overboard, and, at the same time, he could not muster strength to look him in the face.

The short conversation was ended; but now Gavrilo's silence even savored to Tchelkache of the village. He was lost in thoughts of the past and forgot to steer his boat; the waves had turned it and it was now going out to sea.

They seemed to understand that this boat had no aim, and they played with it and lightly tossed it, while their blue fires flamed up under the oars. Before Tchelkache's inward vision, was rapidly unfolded a series of pictures of the past—that far distant past separated from the present by a wall of eleven years of vagrancy. He saw himself again a child, in the village, he saw his mother, red-cheeked, fat, with kind gray eyes,—his father, a giant with a tawny beard and stern countenance,—himself betrothed to Amphissa, black-eyed with a long braid down her back, plump, easy-going, gay. . . And then, himself, a handsome soldier of the guard; later, his father, gray and bent by work, and his mother, wrinkled and bowed. What a merry-making there was at the village when he had returned after the expiration of his service! How proud the father was of his Gregori, the moustached, broad-shouldered soldier, the cock of the village! Memory, that scourge of the unfortunate, brings to life even the stones of the past, and, even to the poison, drunk in former days, adds drops of honey; and all this only to kill man by the consciousness of his faults, and to destroy in his soul all faith in the future by causing him to love the past too well.

Tchelkache was enveloped in a peaceful whiff of natal air that was wafting toward him the sweet words of his mother, the sage counsel of his father, the stern peasant, and many forgotten sounds and savory odors of the earth, frozen as in the springtime, or freshly ploughed, or lastly, covered with young wheat, silky, and green as an emerald. . . Then he felt himself a pitiable, solitary being, gone astray, without attachments and an outcast from the life where the blood in his veins had been formed.

"Hey! Where are we going?" suddenly asked Gavrilo.

Tchelkache started and turned around with the uneasy glance of a wild beast.

"Oh! the devil! Never mind. . . Row more cautiously. . . We're almost there."

"Were you dreaming?" asked Gavrilo, smiling.

Tchelkache looked searchingly at him. The lad was entirely himself again; calm, gay, he even seemed complacent. He was very young, all his life was before him. That was bad! But perhaps the soil would retain him. At this thought, Tchelkache grew sad again, and growled out in reply:

"I'm tired! . . . and the boat rocks!"

"Of course it rocks! So, now, there's no danger of being caught with this?"

Gavrilo kicked the bales.

"No, be quiet. I'm going to deliver them at once and receive the money. Yes!"

"Five hundred?"

"Not less, probably. . ."

"It's a lot! If I had it, poor beggar that I am, I'd soon let it be known."

"At the village? . . ."

"Sure! without delay. . ."

Gavrilo let himself be carried away by his imagination. Tchelkache appeared crushed. His moustache hung down straight; his right side was all wet from the waves, his eyes were sunken in his head and without life. He was a pitiful and dull object. His likeness to a bird of prey had disappeared; self-abasement appeared in the very folds of his dirty blouse.

"I'm tired, worn out!"

"We are landing. . . Here we are."

Tchelkache abruptly turned the boat and guided it toward something black that arose from the water.

The sky was covered with clouds, and a fine, drizzling rain began to fall, pattering joyously on the crests of the waves.

"Stop! . . . Softly!" ordered Tchelkache.

The bow of the boat hit the hull of a vessel.

"Are the devils sleeping?" growled Tchelkache, catching the ropes hanging over the side with his boat-hook. "The ladder isn't lowered. In this rain, besides. . . It couldn't have rained before! Eh! You vermin, there! Eh!"

"Is that you Selkache?" came softly from above.

"Lower the ladder, will you!"

"Good-day, Selkache."

"Lower the ladder, smoky devil!" roared Tchelkache.

"Oh! Isn't he ill-natured to-day. . . Eh! Oh!"

"Go up, Gavrilo!" commanded Tchelkache to his companion.

In a moment they were on the deck, where three dark and bearded individuals were looking over the side at Tchelkache's boat and talking animatedly in a strange and harsh language. A fourth, clad in a long gown, advanced toward Tchelkache, shook his hand in silence and cast a suspicious glance at Gavrilo.

"Get the money ready for to-morrow morning," briefly said Tchelkache. "I'm going to sleep, now. Come Gavrilo. Are you hungry?"

"I'm sleepy," replied Gavrilo,

In five minutes, he was snoring on the dirty deck; Tchelkache sitting beside him, was trying on an old boot that he found lying there. He softly whistled, animated both by sorrow and anger. Then he lay down beside Gavrilo, without removing the boot from his foot, and putting his hands under the back of his neck he carefully examined the deck, working his lips the while.

The boat rocked joyously on the water; the sound of wood creaking dismally was heard, the rain fell softly on the deck, the waves beat against the sides. Everything resounded sadly like the lullaby of a mother who has lost all hope for the happiness of her son.

Tchelkache, with parted lips, raised his head and gazed around him . . . and murmuring a few words, lay down again.

* * * * *

He was the first to awaken, starting up uneasily; then suddenly quieting down he looked at Gavrilo, who was still sleeping. The lad was smiling in his sleep, his round, sun-burned face irradiated with joy.

Tchelkache sighed and climbed up a narrow rope ladder. The opening of the trap-door framed a piece of leaden sky. It was daylight, but the autumn weather was gray and gloomy.

It was two hours before Tchelkache reappeared. His face was red, his moustache curled fiercely upward; his eyes beamed with gaiety and good-nature. He wore high, thick boots, a coat and leather trowsers; he looked like a hunter. His costume, which, although a little worn, was still in good condition and fitted him well, made him appear broader, concealed his too angular lines and gave him a martial air.

"Hey! Youngster, get up!" said he touching Gavrilo with his foot.

The last named started up, and not recognizing him just at first, gazed at him vacantly. Tchelkache burst out laughing.

"How you're gotten up! . . ." finally exclaimed Gavrilo, smiling broadly. "You are a gentleman!"

"We do that quickly here! What a coward you are! Dear, dear! How many times did you make up your mind to die last night, eh? Say. . ."

"But you see, it's the first time I've ever done anything like this! One might lose his soul for the rest of his days!"

"Would you be willing to go again?"

"Again? I must know first what there would be in it for me."

"Two hundred."

"Two hundred, you say? Yes I'd go."

"Stop! . . . And your soul?"

"Perhaps I shouldn't lose it!" said Gavrilo, smiling. "And then one would be a man for the rest of his days!"

Tchelkache burst out laughing. "That's right, but we've joked long enough! Let us row to the shore. Get ready."

"I? Why I'm ready. . ."

They again took their places in the boat. Tchelkache at the helm, Gavrilo rowing.

The gray sky was covered with clouds; the troubled, green sea, played with their craft, tossing it on its still tiny waves that broke over it in a shower of clear, salt drops. Far off, before the prow of the boat, appeared the yellow line of the sandy beach; back of the stern was the free and joyous sea, all furrowed by the troops of waves that ran up and down, already decked in their superb fringe of foam. In the far distance, ships were rocking on the bosom of the sea and, on the left, was a whole forest of masts mingled with the white masses of the houses of the town. Prom there, a dull murmur is borne out to sea and blending with the sound of the waves swelled into rapturous music. Over all stretched a thin veil of mist, widening the distance between the different objects.

"Eh! It'll be rough to-night!" said Tchelkache, nodding his head in the direction of the sea.

"A storm?" asked Gavrilo. He was rowing hard. He was drenched from head to foot by the drops blown by the wind.

"Ehe!" affirmed Tchelkache.

Gavrilo looked at him curiously.

"How much did they give you?" he asked at last, seeing that Tchelkache was not disposed to talk.

"See!" said Tchelkache. He held out toward Gavrilo something that he drew from his pocket.

Gavrilo saw the variegated banknotes, and they assumed in his eyes all the colors of the rainbow.

"Oh! And I thought you were boasting! How much?"

"Five hundred and forty! Isn't that a good haul?"

"Certain!" murmured Gavrilo, following with greedy eyes the five hundred and forty roubles as they again disappeared in the pocket. "Ah! If it was only mine!" He sighed dejectedly.

"We'll have a lark, little one!" enthusiastically exclaimed Tchelkache! "Have no fear: I'll pay you, brother. I'll give you forty rubles! Eh? Are you pleased? Do you want your money now?"

"If you don't mind. Yes, I'll accept it!"

Gavrilo trembled with anticipation; a sharp, burning pain oppressed his breast.

"Ha! ha! ha! Little devil! You'll accept it? Take it, brother, I beg of you! I implore you, take it! I don't know where to put all this money; relieve me, here!"

Tchelkache handed Gavrilo several ten ruble notes. The other took them with a shaking hand, dropped the oars and proceeded to conceal his booty in his blouse, screwing up his eyes greedily, and breathing noisily as though he were drinking something hot. Tchelkache regarded him ironically. Gavrilo seized the oars; he rowed in nervous haste, his eyes lowered, as though he were afraid. His shoulders shook.

"My God, how greedy you are! That's bad. Besides, for a peasant. . ."

"Just think of what one can do with money!" exclaimed Gavrilo, passionately. He began to talk brokenly and rapidly, as though pursuing an idea, and seizing the words on the wing, of life in the country with and without money. "Respect, ease, liberty, gaiety. . ."

Tchelkache listened attentively with a serious countenance and inscrutable eyes. Occasionally, he smiled in a pleased manner.

"Here we are!" he said at last.

A wave seized hold of the boat and landed it high on the sand.

"Ended, ended, quite ended! We must draw the boat up farther, so that it will be out of reach of the tide. They will come after it. And, now, good-bye. The town is eight versts from here. You'll return to town, eh?"

Tchelkache's face still beamed with a slily good-natured smile; he seemed to be planning something pleasant for himself and a surprise for Gavrilo. He put his hand in his pocket and rustled the bank-notes.

"No, I'm not going. . . I. . ."

Gavrilo stifled and choked. He was shaken by a storm of conflicting desires, words and feelings. He burned as though on fire.

Tchelkache gazed at him with astonishment.

"What's the matter with you?" he asked.

"Nothing."

But Gavrilo's face grew red and then ashy pale. The lad moved his feet restlessly as though he would have thrown himself upon Tchelkache, or as though he were torn by Borne secret desire difficult to realize.

His suppressed excitement moved Tchelkache to some apprehension. He wondered what form it would take in breaking out.

Gavrilo gave a laugh, a strange laugh, like a sob. His head was bent, so that Tchelkache could not see the expression of his face; he could only perceive Gavrilo's ears, by turns red and white.

"Go to the devil!" exclaimed Tchelkache, motioning with his hand. "Are you in love with me? Say? Look at you mincing like a young girl. Are you distressed at leaving me? Eh! youngster, speak, or else I'm going!"

"You're going?" cried Gavrilo, in a sonorous voice. The deserted and sandy beach trembled at this cry, and the waves of sand brought by the waves of the sea seemed to shudder. Tchelkache also shuddered. Suddenly Gavrilo darted from his place, and throwing himself at Tchelkache's feet, entwined his legs with his arms and drew him toward him. Tchelkache tottered, sat down heavily on the sand, and gritting his teeth, brandished his long arm and closed fist in the air. But before he had time to strike, he was stopped by the troubled and suppliant look of Gavrilo.

"Friend! Give me . . . that money! Give it to me, in the name of Heaven. What need have you of it? It is the earnings of one night . . . a single night . . . And it would take me years to get as much as that. . . Give it to me. . . . I'll pray for you . . . all my life . . . in three churches . . . for the safety of your soul. You'll throw it to the winds, and I'll give it to the earth. Oh! give me that money. What will you do with it, say? Do you care about it as much as that? One night . . . and you are rich! Do a good deed! You are lost, you! . . . You'll never come back again to the way, while I! . . . Ah! give it to me!"

Tchelkache frightened, astonished and furious threw himself backward, still seated on the sand, and leaning on his two hands silently gazed at him, his eyes starting from their orbits; the lad leaned his head on his knees and gasped forth his supplications. Tchelkache finally pushed him away, jumped to his feet, and thrusting his hand into his pocket threw the multi-colored bills at Gavrilo.

"There, dog, swallow them!" he cried trembling with mingled feelings of anger, pity and hate for this greedy slave. Now that he had thrown him the money, he felt himself a hero. His eyes, his whole person, beamed with conscious pride.

"I meant to have given you more. I pitied you yesterday. I thought of the village. I said to myself: 'I'll help this boy.' I was waiting to see what you'd do, whether you'd ask me or not. And now, see! tatterdemalion, beggar, that you are! . . . Is it right to work oneself up to such a state for money . . . to suffer like that? Imbeciles, greedy devils who forget . . . who would sell themselves for five kopeks, eh?"

"Friend . . . Christ's blessing on you! What is this? What? Thousands? . . . I'm a rich man, now!" screamed Gavrilo, in a frenzy of delight, hiding the money in his blouse. "Ah! dear man! I shall, never forget this! never! And I'll beg my wife and children to pray for you."

Tchelkache listened to these cries of joy, gazed at this face, irradiated and disfigured by the passion of covetousness; he felt that he himself, the thief and vagabond, freed from all restraining influence, would never become so rapacious, so vile, so lost to all decency. Never would he sink so low as that! Lost in these reflections, which brought to him the consciousness of his liberty and his audacity, he remained beside Gavrilo on the lonely shore.

"You have made me happy!" cried Gavrilo, seizing Tchelkache's hand and laying it against his cheek.

Tchelkache was silent and showed his teeth like a wolf. Gavrilo continued to pour out his heart.

"What an idea that was of mine! We were rowing here . . . I saw the money . . . I said to myself:

"Suppose I were to give him . . . give you . . . a blow with the oar . . . just one! The money would be mine; as for him, I'd throw him in the sea . . . you, you understand? Who would ever notice his disappearance? And if you were found, no inquest would be made: who, how, why had you been killed? You're not the kind of man for whom any stir would be made! You're of no use on the earth! Who would take your part? That's the way it would be! Eh?"

"Give back that money!" roared Tchelkache, seizing Gavrilo by the throat.

Gavrilo struggled, once, twice . . . but Tchelkache's other arm entwined itself like a serpent around him . . . a noise of tearing linen,—and Gavrilo slipped to the ground with bulging eyes, catching at the air with his hands and waving his legs. Tchelkache, erect, spare, like a wild beast, showed his teeth wickedly and laughed harshly, while his moustache worked nervously on his sharp, angular face. Never, in his whole life, had he been so deeply wounded, and never had his anger been so great.

"Well! Are you happy, now?" asked he, still laughing, of Gavrilo, and turning his back to him, he walked away in the direction of the town.

But he had hardly taken two steps when Gavrilo, crouching like a cat, threw a large, round stone at him, crying furiously:

"O—one!"

Tchelkache groaned, raised his hands to the back of his neck and stumbled forward, then turned toward Gavrilo and fell face downward on the sand. He moved a leg, tried to raise his head and stiffened, vibrating like a stretched cord. At this, Gavrilo began to run, to run far away, yonder, to where the shadow of that ragged cloud overhung the misty steppe. The murmuring waves, coursing over the sands, joined him and ran on and on, never stopping. The foam hissed, the spray flew through the air.

The rain fell. Slight at first, it soon came down thickly, heavily and came from the sky in slender streams. They crossed, forming a net that soon shut off the distance on land and water. For a long time there was nothing to be seen but the rain and this long body lying on the sand beside the sea . . . But suddenly, behold Gavrilo coming from out the rain, running; he flew like a bird. He went up to Tchelkache, fell upon his knees before him, and tried to turn him over. His hand sank into a sticky liquid, warm and red. He trembled and drew back, pale and distracted.

"Get up, brother!" he whispered amid the noise of the falling rain into the ear of Tchelkache.

Tchelkache came to himself and, repulsing Gavrilo, said in a hoarse voice:

"Go away!"

"Forgive me, brother: I was tempted by the devil . . ." continued Gavrilo, trembling and kissing Tchelkache's hand.

"Go, go away!" growled the other.

"Absolve my sin! Friend . . . forgive me!"

"Go, go to the devil!" suddenly cried out Tchelkache, sitting up on the sand. His face was pale, threatening; his clouded eyes closed as though he were very sleepy . . . "What do you want, now? You've finished your business . . . go! Off with you!"

He tried to kick Gavrilo, prostrated by grief, but failed, and would have fallen if Gavrilo hadn't supported him with his shoulders. Tchelkache's face was now on a level with Gavrilo's. Both were pale, wretched and terrifying.

"Fie!"

Tchelkache spat in the wide opened eyes of his employe.

The other humbly wiped them with his sleeve, and murmured:

"Do what you will . . . I'll not say one word. Pardon me, in the name of Heaven!"

"Fool, you don't even know how to steal!" cried Tchelkache, contemptuously. He tore his shirt under his waistcoat and, gritting his teeth in silence, began to bandage his head.

"Have you taken the money?" he asked, at last.

"I haven't taken it, brother; I don't want it! It brings bad luck!"

Tchelkache thrust his hand into his waistcoat pocket, withdrew the package of bills, put one of them in his pocket and threw all the rest at Gavrilo.

"Take that and be off!"

"I cannot take it . . . I cannot! Forgive me!"

"Take it, I tell you!" roared Tchelkache, rolling his eyes frightfully.

"Pardon me! When you have forgiven me I'll take it," timidly said Gavrilo, falling on the wet sand at Tchelkache's feet.

"You lie, fool, you'll take it at once!" said Tchelkache, confidently, and raising his head, by a painful effort, he thrust the money before his face. "Take it, take it! You haven't worked for nothing! Don't be ashamed of having failed to assassinate a man! No one will claim anyone like me. You'll be thanked, on the contrary, when it's learned what you've done. There, take it! No one'll know what you've done and yet it deserves some reward! Here it is!"

Gavrilo saw that Tchelkache was laughing, and he felt relieved. He held the money tightly in his hand.

"Brother! Will you forgive me? Won't you do it? Say?" he supplicated tearfully.

"Little brother!" mimicked Tchelkache, rising on his tottering limbs. "Why should I pardon you? There's no occasion for it. To-day it's you, to-morrow it'll be me . . ."

"Ah! brother, brother!" sighed Gavrilo, sorrowfully, shaking his head.

Tchelkache was standing before him, smiling strangely; the cloth wrapped around his head, gradually reddening, resembled a Turkish head-dress.

The rain fell in torrents. The sea complained dully and the waves beat angrily against the beach.

The two men were silent.

"Good-bye!" said Tchelkache, with cold irony.

He staggered, his legs trembled, and he carried his head oddly, as though he was afraid of losing it.

"Pardon me, brother!" again repeated Gavrilo.

"It's nothing!" drily replied Tchelkache, as he supported his head with his left hand and gently pulled his moustache with his right.

Gavrilo stood gazing after him until he had disappeared in the rain that still fell in fine, close drops, enveloping the steppe in a mist as impenetrable and gray as steel.

Then Gavrilo took off his wet cap, made the sign of the cross, looked at the money pressed tightly in his hand and drew a long, deep sigh; he concealed his booty in his blouse and began to walk, taking long strides, in the opposite direction to that in which Tchelkache had gone.

The sea thundered, threw great heavy waves upon the sand and broke them into foam and spray. The rain lashed the sea and land pitilessly; the wind roared. All the air around was filled with plaints, cries and dull sounds. The rain masked sea and sky. . .

The rain and the breaking waves soon washed away the red spot where Tchelkache had been struck to the ground; they soon effaced his footprints and those of the lad on the sand, and the lonely beach was left without the slightest trace of the little drama that had been played between these two men.

MALVA

BY MAXIME GORKY

The sea laughed.

It trembled at the warm and light breath of the wind and became covered with tiny wrinkles that reflected the sun in blinding fashion and laughed at the sky with its thousands of silvery lips. In the deep space between sea and sky buzzed the deafening and joyous sound of the waves chasing each other on the flat beach of the sandy promontory. This noise and brilliancy of sunlight, reverberated a thousand times by the sea, mingled harmoniously in ceaseless and joyous agitation. The sky was glad to shine; the sea was happy to reflect the glorious light.

The wind caressed the powerful and satin-like breast of the sea, the sun heated it with its rays and it sighed as if fatigued by these ardent caresses; it filled the burning air with the salty aroma of its emanations. The green waves, coursing up the yellow sand, threw on the beach the white foam of their luxurious crests which melted with a gentle murmur, and wet it.

At intervals along the beach, scattered with shells and sea weed, were stakes of wood driven into the sand and on which hung fishing nets, drying and casting shadows as fine as cobwebs. A few large boats and a small one were drawn up beyond high-water mark, and the waves as they ran up towards them seemed as if they were calling to them. Gaffs, oars, coiled ropes, baskets and barrels lay about in disorder and amidst it all was a cabin built of yellow branches, bark and matting. Above the general chaos floated a red rag at the extremity of a tall mast.

Under the shade of a boat lay Vassili Legostev, the watchman at this outpost of the Grebentchikov fishing grounds. Lying on his stomach, his head resting on his hands, he was gazing fixedly out to sea, where away in the distance danced a black spot. Vassili saw with satisfaction that it grew larger and was drawing nearer.

Screwing up his eyes on account of the glare caused by the reflection on the water, he grunted with pleasure and content. Malva was coming. A few minutes more and she would be there, laughing so heartily as to strain every stitch of her well-filled bodice. She would throw her robust and gentle arms around him and kiss him, and in that rich sonorous voice that startles the sea gulls would give him the news of what was going on yonder. They would make a good fish soup together, and drink brandy as they chatted and caressed each other. That is how they spent every Sunday and holiday. And at daylight he would row her back over the sea in the sharp morning air. Malva, still nodding with sleep, would hold the tiller and he would watch her as he pulled. She was amusing at those times, funny and charming both, like a cat which had eaten well. Sometimes she would slip from her seat and roll herself up at the bottom of the boat like a ball.

As Vassili watched the little black spot grow larger it seemed to him that Malva was not alone in the boat. Could Serejka have come along with her? Vassili moved heavily on the sand, sat up, shaded his eyes with his hands, and with a show of ill humor began to strain his eyes to see who was coming. No, the man rowing was not Serejka. He rows strong but clumsily. If Serejka were rowing Malva would not take the trouble to hold the rudder.

"Hey there!" cried Vassili impatiently.

The sea gulls halted in their flight and listened.

"Hallo! Hallo!" came back from the boat. It was Malva's sonorous voice.

"Who's with you?"

A laugh replied to him.

"Jade!" swore Vassili under his breath.

He spat on the ground with vexation.

He was puzzled. While he rolled a cigarette he examined the neck and back of the rower who was rapidly drawing nearer. The sound of the water when the oars struck it resounded in the still air, and the sand crunched under the watchman's bare feet as he stamped about in his impatience.

"Who's with you?" he cried, when he could discern the familiar smile on Malva's pretty plump face.

"Wait. You'll know him all right," she replied laughing.

The rower turned on his seat and, also laughing, looked at Vassili.

The watchman frowned. It seemed to him that he knew the fellow.

"Pull harder!" commanded Malva.

The stroke was so vigorous that the boat was carried up the beach on a wave, fell over on one side and then righted itself while the wave rolled back laughing into the sea. The rower jumped out on the beach, and going up to Vassili said:

"How are you, father?"

"Iakov!" cried Vassili, more surprised than pleased.

They embraced three times. Afterwards Vassili's stupor became mingled with both joy and uneasiness. The watchman stroked his blond beard with one hand and with the other gesticulated:

"I knew something was up; my heart told me so. So it was you! I kept asking myself if it was Serejka. But I saw it was not Serejka. How did you come here?"

Vassili would have liked to look at Malva, but his son's rollicking eyes were upon him and he did not dare. The pride he felt at having a son so strong and handsome struggled in him with the embarrassment caused by the presence of Malva. He shuffled about and kept asking Iakov one question after another, often without waiting for a reply. His head felt awhirl, and he felt particularly uneasy when he heard Malva say in a mocking tone.

"Don't skip about—for joy. Take him to the cabin and give him something to eat."

The father examined his son from head to foot. On the latter's lips hovered that cunning smile Vassili knew so well. Malva turned her green eyes from the father to the son and munched melon seeds between her small white teeth. Iakov smiled and for a few seconds, which were painful to Vassili, all three were silent.

"I'll come back in a moment," said Vassili suddenly going towards the cabin. "Don't stay there in the sun, I'm going to fetch some water. We'll make some soup. I'll give you some fish soup, Iakov."

He seized a saucepan that was lying on the ground and disappeared behind the fishing nets.

Malva and the peasant followed him.

"Well, my fine young fellow, I brought you to your father, didn't I?" said Malva, brushing up against Iakov's robust figure.

He turned towards her his face framed in its curled blond beard, and with a brilliant gleam in his eyes said:

"Yes, here we are—It's fine here, isn't it? What a stretch of sea!"

"The sea is great. Has the old man changed much?"

"No, not much. I expected to find him more grey. He's still pretty solid."

"How long is it since you saw him?"

"About five years. I was nearly seventeen when he left the village."

They entered the cabin, the air of which was suffocating from the heat and the odor of cooking fish. They sat down. Between them there was a roughly-hewn oak table. They looked at each other for a long time without speaking.

"So you want to work here?" said Malva at last.

"I don't know. If I find something, I'll work."

"You'll find work," replied Malva with assurance, examining him critically with her green eyes.

He paid no attention to her, and with his sleeve wiped away the perspiration that covered his face.

She suddenly began to laugh.

"Your mother probably sent messages for your father by you?"

Iakov gave a shrug of ill humor and replied:

"Of course. What if she did?"

"Oh, nothing."

And she laughed the louder.

Her laugh displeased Iakov. He paid no attention to her and thought of his mother's instructions. When she accompanied him to the end of the village she had said quickly, blinking her eyes:

"In Christ's name, Iakov say to him: 'Father, mother is alone yonder. Five years have gone by and she is always alone. She is getting old.' Tell him that, Iakov, my little Iakov, for the love of God. Mother will soon be an old woman. She's always alone, always at work. In Christ's name, tell him that."

And she had wept silently, hiding her face in her apron.

Iakov had not pitied her then, but he did now. And his face took on a hard expression before Malva, as if he were about to abuse her.

"Here I am!" cried Vassili, bursting in on them with a wriggling fish in one hand and a knife in the other.

He had not got over his uneasiness, but had succeeded in dissimulating it deep within him. Now he looked at his guests with serenity and good nature; only his manner was more agitated than usual.

"I'll make a bit of a fire in a minute, and we'll talk. Why, Iakov, what a fine fellow you've grown!"

Again he disappeared.

Malva went on munching her melon seeds. She stared familiarly at Iakov. He tried not to meet her eyes, although he would have liked to, and he thought to himself:

"Life must come easy here. People seem to eat as much as they want to. How strong she is and father, too!"

Then intimidated by the silence, he said aloud:

"I forgot my bag in the boat. I'll go and get it."

Iakov rose leisurely and went out. Vassili appeared a moment later. He bent down towards Malva and said rapidly with anger:

"What did you want to bring him for? What shall I tell him about you?"

"What's that to me? Am I afraid of him? Or of you?" she asked, closing her green eyes with disdain. Then she laughed: "How you went on when you saw him. It was so funny!"

"Funny, eh?"

The sand crunched under Iakov's steps and they had to suspend their conversation. Iakov had brought a bag which he threw into a corner. He cast a hostile look at the young woman.

She went on munching her seeds. Vassili, seating himself on the woodbin, said with a forced smile:

"What made you think of coming?"

"Why, I just came. We wrote you."

"When? I haven't received any letter."

"Really? We wrote often."

"The letter must have got lost," said Vassili regretfully. "It always does when it's important."

"So you don't know how things are at home?" asked Iakov, suspiciously.

"How should I know? I received no letter."

Then Iakov told him that the horse was dead, that all the corn had been eaten before the beginning of February, and that he himself had been unable to find any work. Hay was also short, and the cow had almost perished from hunger. They had managed as best they could until April and then they decided that Iakov should join the father far away and work three months with him. That is what they had written. Then they sold three sheep, bought flour and hay and Iakov had started.

"How is that possible?" cried Vassali. "I sent you some money."

"Your money didn't go far. We repaired the cottage, we had to marry sister off and I bought a plough. You know five years is a long time."

"Hum," said Vassili, "wasn't it enough? What a tale of woe! Ah, there's my soup boiling over!"

He rose and stooping before the fire on which was the saucepan, Vassili meditated while throwing the scum into the flame. Nothing in his son's recital had touched him particularly, and he felt irritated against his wife and Iakov. He had sent them a great deal of money during the last five years, and yet they had not been able to manage. If Malva had not been present he would have told his son what he thought about it. Iakov was smart enough to leave the village on his own responsibility and without the father's permission, but he had not been able to get a living out of the soil. Vassili sighed as he stirred the soup, and as he watched the blue flames he thought of his son and Malva. Henceforward, he thought, his life would be less agreeable, less free. Iakov had surely guessed what Malva was.

Meanwhile Malva, in the cabin, was trying to arouse the rustic with her bold eyes.

"Perhaps you left a girl in the village?" she asked suddenly.

"Perhaps," he responded surlily.

Inwardly he was abusing Malva.

"Is she pretty?" she asked with indifference.

Iakov made no reply.

"Why don't you answer? Is she better looking than I, or no?"

He looked at her in spite of himself. Her cheeks were sunburnt and plump, her lips red and tempting and now, parted in a malicious smile, showing the white even teeth, they seemed to tremble. Her bust was full and firm under a pink cotton waist that set off to advantage her trim waist and well-rounded arms. But he did not like her green and cynical eyes.

"Why do you talk like that?" he asked.

He sighed without reason and spoke in a beseeching tone, yet he wanted to speak brutally to her.

"How shall I talk?" she asked laughing.

"There you are, laughing—at what?"

"At you—."

"What have I done to you?" he said with irritation. And once more he lowered his eyes under her gaze.

She made no reply.

Iakov understood her relations towards his father perfectly well and that prevented him from expressing himself freely. He was not surprised. It would have been difficult for a man like his father to have been long without a companion.

"The soup is ready," announced Vassili, at the threshold of the cabin. "Get the spoons, Malva."

When she found the spoons she said she must go down to the sea to wash them.

The father and son watched her as she ran down the sands and both were silent.

"Where did you meet her?" asked Vassili, finally.

"I went to get news of you at the office. She was there. She said to me: 'Why go on foot along the sand? Come in the boat. I'm going there.' And so we started."

"And—what do you think of her?"

"Not bad," said Iakov, vaguely, blinking his eyes.

"What could I do?" asked Vassili. "I tried at first. But it was impossible. She mends my clothes and so on. Besides it's as easy to escape from death as from a woman when once she's after you."

"What's it to me?" said Iakov. "It's your affair. I'm not your judge."

Malva now returned with the spoons, and they sat down to dinner. They ate without talking, sucking the bones noisily and spitting them out on the sand, near the door. Iakov literally devoured his food, which seemed to please Malva vastly; she watched with tender interest his sunburnt cheeks extend and his thick humid lips moving quickly. Vassili was not hungry. He tried, however, to appear absorbed in the meal so as to be able to watch Malva and Iakov at his ease.

After awhile, when Iakov had eaten his fill he said he was sleepy.

"Lie down here," said Vassili. "We'll wake you up."

"I'm willing," said Iakov, sinking down on a coil of rope. "And what will you do?"

Embarrassed by his son's smile, Vassili left the cabin hastily, Malva frowned and replied to Iakov:

"What's that to you? Learn to mind your own business, my lad."

Then she went out.

Iakov turned over and went to sleep.

Vassili had fixed three stakes in the sand, and with a piece of matting had rigged up a shelter from the sun. Then he lay down flat on his back and contemplated the sky. When Malva came up and dropped on the sand by his side he turned towards her with vexation plainly written on his face.

"Well, old man," she said laughing, "you don't seem pleased to see your son."

"He mocks me. And why? Because of you," replied Vassili testily.

"Oh, I am sorry. What can we do? I mustn't come here again, eh? All right. I'll not come again."

"Siren that you are! Ah, you women! He mocks me and you too—and yet you are what I have dearest to me."

He moved away from her and was silent. Squatting on the sand, with her legs drawn up to her chin, Malva balanced herself gently to and fro, idly gazing with her green eyes over the dazzling joyous sea, and she smiled with triumph as all women do when they understand the power of their beauty.

"Why don't you speak?" asked Vassili.

"I'm thinking," said Malva. Then after a pause she added:

"Your son's a fine fellow."

"What's that to you?" cried Vassili, jealously.

"Who knows?"

He glanced at her suspiciously. "Take care," he said, menacingly. "Don't play the imbecile. I'm a patient man, but I mustn't be crossed."

He ground his teeth and clenched his fists.

"Don't frighten me, Vassili," she said indifferently, without looking up at him.

"Well, stop your joking."

"Don't try to frighten me."

"I'll soon make you dance if you begin any foolishness."

"Would you beat me?"

She went up to him and gazed with curiosity at his frowning face.

"One would think you were a countess. Yes, I would beat you."

"Yet I'm not your wife," said Malva, calmly. "You have been accustomed to beat your wife for nothing, and you imagine that you can do the same with me. No, I am free. I belong only to myself, and I am afraid of no one. But you are afraid of your son, and now you dare threaten me."

She shook her head with disdain. Her careless manner cooled Vassili's anger. He had never seen her look so beautiful.

"I have something else to tell you," she went on. "You boasted to Serejka that I could no more get along without you than without bread, and that I cannot live without you. You are mistaken. Perhaps it is not you that I love and not for you that I come. Perhaps I love the peace of this deserted beach. (Here she made a wide gesture with her arms.) Perhaps I love these lonely sands, with their vast stretch of sea and sky, and to be away from vile beings. Because you are here is nothing to me. If this were Serejka's place I should come here. If your son lived here, I should come too. It would be better still if no one were here, for I am disgusted with you all. But if I take it into my head one day—beautiful as I am—I can always choose a man, and one who'll please me better than you."

"So, so!" hissed Vassili, furiously, and he seized her by the throat. "So that's your game, is it?"

He shook her, and she did not strive to get away from his grasp, although her face was congested and her eyes bloodshot. She merely placed her two hands on the rough hands that were around her throat.

"Ah, now I know you!" Vassili was hoarse with rage. "And yet you said you loved me, and you kissed me and caressed me? Ah, I'll show you!"

Holding her down to the ground, he struck her repeatedly with his clenched fist. Finally, fatigued with the exertion, he pushed her away from him crying:

"There, serpent. Now you've got what you deserved."

Without a complaint, silent and calm, Malva fell back on her back, all crumpled, red and still beautiful. Her green eyes watched him furtively under the lashes, and burned with a cold flame full of hatred, but he, gasping with excitement and satisfied with the punishment he had inflicted, did not notice the look, and when he stooped down towards her to see if she was crying, she smiled up at him gently.

He looked at her, not understanding and not knowing what to do next. Should he beat her again? But his fury was appeased, and he had no desire to recommence.

"How you love me!" she whispered.

Vassili felt hot all over.

"All right! all right! the devil take you," he said gloomily. "Are you satisfied now?"

"Was I not foolish, Vassili? I thought you no longer loved me! I said to myself, 'now his son is here he will neglect me for him.'"

And she burst out laughing, a strange forced laugh.

"Foolish girl!" said Vassili, smiling in spite of himself.

He felt himself at fault, and was sorry for her, but remembering what she had said, he went on crossly:

"My son has nothing to do with it. If I beat you it was your own fault. Why did you cross me?"

"I did it on purpose to try you."

And purring like a cat she rubbed herself against his shoulder.

He glanced furtively towards the cabin and bending down embraced the young woman.

"To try me?" he repeated. "As if you wanted to do that? You see the result?"

"Oh, that's nothing!" said Malva, half closing her eyes. "I'm not angry. You beat me only because you loved me. You'll make it up to me."

She gave him a long look, trembled and lowering her voice repeated:

"Oh, yes, you'll make it up to me."

Vassili interpreted her words in a sense agreeable to him.

"How?" he asked.

"You'll see," replied Malva calmly, very calmly, but her lips trembled.

"Ah, my darling!" cried Vassili, clasping her close in his arms. "Do you know that since I have beaten you I love you better." Her head fell back on his shoulders and he placed his lips on her trembling mouth.

The sea gulls whirled about over their heads uttering hoarse cries. From the distance came the regular and gentle splash of the tiny waves breaking on the sand.

When, at last, they broke from their long embrace, Malva sat up on Vassili's knee. The peasant's face, tanned by wind and sun, was bent close to hers and his great blond beard tickled her neck. The young woman was motionless;

- 56 -

only the gradual and regular rise and fall of her bosom showed her to be alive. Vassili's eyes wandered in turn from the sea to this woman by his side. He told Malva how tired he was of living alone and how painful were his sleepless nights filled with gloomy thoughts. Then he kissed her again on the mouth with the same sound that he might have made in chewing a hot piece of meat.

They stayed there three hours in this way, and finally, when he saw the sun setting, Vassili said with a bored look:

"I must go and make some tea. Our guest will soon he awake."

Malva rose with the indolent gesture of a languorous cat, and with a gesture of regret he started towards the cabin. Through her half-open lids the young woman watched him as he moved away, and sighed as people sigh when they have borne too heavy a burden.

* * * * *

Fifteen days later it was again Sunday and again Vassili Legostev, stretched out on the sand near his hut, was gazing out to sea, waiting for Malva. And the deserted sea laughed, playing with the reflections of the sun, and legions of waves were born to run on the sand, deposit the foam of their crests and return to the sea, where they melted.

All was as before. Only Vassili, who the last time awaited her coming with peaceful security, was now filled with impatience. Last Sunday she had not come; to-day she would surely come. He did not doubt it for a moment, but he wanted to see her as soon as possible. Iakov, at least, would not be there to embarrass them. The day before yesterday, as he passed with the other fishermen, he said he would go to town on Sunday to buy a blouse. He had found work at fifteen roubles a month.

Except for the gulls, the sea was still deserted. The familiar little black spot did not appear,

"Ah, you're not coming!" said Vassili, with ill humor. "All right, don't. I don't want you."

And he spat with disdain in the direction of the water.

The sea laughed.

"If, at least, Serejka would come," he thought. And he tried to think only of Serejka. "What a good-for-nothing the fellow is! Robust, able to read, seen the world—but what a drunkard! Yet good company. One can't feel dull in his company. The women are mad for him; all run after him. Malva's the only one that keeps aloof. No, no sign of her! What a cursed woman! Perhaps she's angry because I beat her."

Thus, thinking of his son, of Serejka, but more often of Malva, Vassili paced up and down the sandy beach, turning every now and then to look anxiously out to sea. But Malva did not come.

This is what had happened.

Iakov rose early, and on going down to the beach as usual to wash himself, he saw Malva. She was seated on the bow of a large fishing boat anchored in the surf and letting her bare feet hang, sat combing her damp hair.

Iakov stopped to watch her.

"Have you had a bath?" he cried.

She turned to look at him, and glanced down at her feet: then, continuing to comb herself, she replied:

"Yes, I took a bath. Why are you up so early?"

"Aren't you up early?"

"I am not an example for you. If you did all I do, you'd be in all kinds of trouble."

"Why do you always wish to frighten me?" he asked.

"And you, why do you make eyes at me?"

Iakov had no recollection of having looked at her more than at the other women on the fishing grounds, but now he said to her suddenly:

"Because you are so—appetizing."

"If your father heard you, he'd give you an appetite! No, my lad, don't run after me, because I don't want to be between you and Vassili. You understand?"

"What have I done?" asked Iakov. "I haven't touched you."

"You daren't touch me," retorted Malva.

There was such a contemptuous tone in her voice that he resented this.

"So I dare not?" he replied, climbing up on the boat and seating himself at her side.

"No, you dare not."

"And if I touch you?"

"Try!"

"What would you do?"

"I'd give you such a box on the ear that you would fall into the water."

"Let's see you do it"

"Touch me if you dare!"

Throwing his arm around her waist, he pressed her to his breast.

"Here I am. Now box my ears."

"Let me be, Iakov," she said, quickly, trying to disengage herself from his arms which trembled.

"Where is the punishment you promised me?"

"Let go or take care!"

"Oh, stop your threats—luscious strawberry that you are!"

He drew her to him and pressed his thick lips into her sunburnt cheek.

She gave a wild laugh of defiance, seized Iakov's arms and suddenly, with a quick movement of her whole body threw herself forward. They fell into the water enlaced, forming a single heavy mass, and disappeared under the splashing foam. Then from beneath the agitated water Iakov appeared, looking half drowned. Malva, at his side swimming like a fish, eluded his grasp, and tried to prevent him regaining the boat. Iakov struggled desperately, striking the water and roaring like a walrus, while Malva, screaming with laughter, swam round and round him, throwing the salt water in his face, and then diving to avoid his vigorous blows.

At last he caught her and pulled her under the water, and the waves passed over both their heads. Then they came to the surface again both panting with the exertion. Thus they played like two big fish until, finally, tired out and full of salt water, they climbed up the beach and sat down in the sun to dry.

Malva laughed and twisted her hair to get the water out.

The day was growing. The fishermen, after their night of heavy slumber, were emerging from their huts, one by one. From the distance all looked alike. One began to strike blows on an empty barrel at regular intervals. Two women were heard quarrelling. Dogs barked.

"They are getting up," said Iakov. "And I wanted to start to town early. I've lost time with you."

"One does nothing good in my company," she said, half in jest, half seriously.

"What a habit you have of scaring people," replied Iakov.

"You'll see when your father—."

This allusion to his father angered him.

"What about my father? I'm not a boy. And I'm not blind, either. He's not a saint, either; he deprives himself of nothing. If you don't mind I'll steal you from my father."

"You?"

"Do you think I wouldn't dare?"

"Really?"

"Now, look you," he began furiously, "don't defy me. I—."

"What now?" she asked with indifference.

"Nothing."

He turned away with a determined look on his face.

"How brave you are," she said, tauntingly. "You remind me of the inspector's little dog. At a distance he barks and threatens to bite, but when you get near him he puts his tail between his legs and runs away."

"All right," cried Iakov, angrily. "Wait! you'll see what I am."

Advancing towards them came a sunburnt, tattered and muscular-looking individual. He wore a ragged red shirt, his trousers were full of holes, and his feet were bare. His face was covered with freckles and he had big saucy blue eyes and an impertinent turned-up nose. When he came up he stopped and made a grimace.

"Serejka drank yesterday, and today Serejka's pocket is empty. Lend me twenty kopeks. I'll not return them."

Iakov burst out laughing; Malva smiled.

"Give me the money," went on the tramp. "I'll marry you for twenty kopeks if you like."

"You're an odd fellow," said Iakov, "are you a priest?"

"Imbecile question," replied Serejka. "Wasn't I servant to a priest at Ouglitch?"

"I don't want to get married," said Iakov.

"Give the money all the same, and I won't tell your father you're paying court to his queen," replied Serejka, passing his tongue over his dry and cracked lips.

Iakov did not want to give twenty kopeks, but they had warned him to be on his guard when dealing with Serejka, and to put up with his whims. The tramp never demanded much, but if he was refused he spread evil tales about you or else he would beat you. So Iakov, sighing, put his hand in his pocket.

"That's right," said Serejka, with a tone of encouragement, and he sat down beside them on the sand. "Always do what I tell you and you'll be happy. And you," he went on, turning to Malva—"when are you going to marry me? Better be quick. I don't like to wait long."

"You are too ragged. Begin by sewing up your holes and then we'll see," replied Malva.

Serejka regarded his rents with a reproachful air and shook his head.

"Give me one of your skirts, that'll be better."

"Yes, I can," said Malva, laughing.

"I'm serious. You must have an old one you don't want."

"You'd do better to buy yourself a pair of trousers."

"I prefer to drink the money."

Serejka rose and, jingling his twenty kopeks, shuffled off, followed by a strange smile from Malva.

When he was some distance away, Iakov said:

"In our village such a braggart would goon have been put in his place. Here, every one seems afraid of him."

Malva looked at Iakov and replied, disdainfully:

"You don't know his worth."

"There's nothing to know. He's worth five kopeks a hundred."

She did not reply, but watched the play of the waves as they chased one after the other, swaying the fishing boat. The mast inclined now to right, now to left, and the bow rose and then fell suddenly, striking the water with a loud splash.

"Why don't you go?" asked Malva.

"Where?" he asked.

"You wanted to go to town."

"I shan't go now."

"Well, go to your father's."

"And you?"

"What?"

"Shall you go, too?"

"No."

"Then I shan't either."

"Are you going to stay round me all day?"

"I don't want your company so much as that," replied Iakov, offended.

He rose and moved away. But he was mistaken in saying that he did not need her, for when away from her he felt lonely. A strange feeling had come to him after their conversation, a secret desire to protest against the father. Only yesterday this feeling had not existed, nor even to-day, before he saw Malva. Now it seemed to him that his father embarrassed him and stood in his way, although he was far away over the sea yonder, on a narrow tongue of sand almost invisible to the eye. Then it seemed to him, too, that Malva was afraid of the father; if she were not afraid she would talk differently. Now she was missing in his life while only that morning he had not thought of her.

And so he wandered for several hours along the beach, stopping here and there to chat with fishermen he knew. At noon he took a siesta under the shade of an upturned boat. When he awoke he took another stroll and came across Malva far from the fishing ground, reading a tattered book under the shade of the willows.

She looked up at Iakov and smiled.

"Ah, there you are," he said, sitting down beside her.

"Have you been looking for me long?" she asked, demurely.

"Looking for you? What an idea?" replied Iakov, who was only just beginning to realize that it was the truth.

"Do you know how to read?" she asked.

"Yes—I used to, but I've forgotten everything."

"So have I."

"Why didn't you go to the headland to-day?" asked Iakov, suddenly.

"What's that to you?"

Iakov plucked a leaf and chewed it.

"Listen," he said in a low tone and drawing near her. "Listen to what I'm going to say. I'm young and I love you."

"You're a silly lad, very silly," said Malva, shaking her head.

"I may be a fool," cried Iakov, passionately. "But I love you, I love you."

"Be silent! Go away!"

"Why?"

"Because."

"Don't be obstinate." He took her gently by the shoulders. "Can't you understand?"

"Go away, Iakov," she cried, severely. "Go away!"

"Oh, if that's the tone you take I don't care a rap. You're not the only woman here. You imagine that you are better than the others."

She made no reply, rose and brushed the dust off her skirt.

"Come," she said.

And they went back to the fishing grounds side by side.

They walked slowly on account of the soft sand. Suddenly, as they were nearing the boats, Iakov stopped short and seized Malva by the arms.

"Are you driving me desperate on purpose? Why do you play with me like this?" he demanded.

"Leave me alone, I tell you," she said, calmly disengaging herself from his grasp.

Serejka appeared from behind a boat. He shook his fist at the couple, and said, threateningly:

"So, that's how you go off together. Vassili shall know of this."

"Go to the devil, all of you!" cried Malva. And she left them, disappearing among the boats.

Iakov stood facing Serejka, and looked him square in the face. Serejka boldly returned the stare and so they remained for a minute or two, like two rams ready to charge on each other. Then without a word each turned away and went off in a different direction.

The sea was calm and crimson with the rays of the setting sun. A confused sound hovered over the fishing ground. The voice of a drunken woman sang hysterically words devoid of sense.

* * * * *

In the dawn's pure light the sea still slumbered, reflecting the pearl-like clouds. On the headland a party of fishermen still only half awake moved slowly about, getting ready the rigging of their boat.

Serejka, bareheaded and tattered as usual, stood in the bow hurrying the men on with a hoarse voice, the result of his drunken orgy of the previous night.

"Where are the oars, Vassili?"

Vassili, moody as a dark autumn day, was arranging the net at the bottom of the boat. Serejka watched him and, when he looked his way, smacked his lips, signifying that he wanted to drink.

"Have you any brandy," he asked.

"Yes," growled Vassili.

"Good. I'll take a nip when they've gone."

"Is all ready?" cried the fishermen.

"Let go!" commanded Serejka, jumping to the ground. "Be careful. Go far out so as not to entangle the net."

The big boat slid down the greased planks to the water, and the fishermen, jumping in as it went, seized the oars, ready to strike the water directly she was afloat. Then with a big splash the graceful bark forged ahead through the great plain of luminous water.

"Why didn't you come Sunday?" said Vassili, as the two men went back to the cabin.

"I couldn't."

"You were drunk?"

"No, I was watching your son and his step-mother," said Serejka, phlegmatically.

"A new worry on your shoulders," said Vassili, sarcastically and with a forced smile. "They are only children." He was tempted to learn where and how Serejka had seen Malva and Iakov the day before, but he was ashamed.

"Why don't you ask news of Malva?" asked Serejka, as he gulped down a glass of brandy.

"What do I care what she does?" replied Vassili, with indifference, although he trembled with a secret presentiment.

"As she didn't come Sunday, you should ask what she was doing. I know you are jealous, you old dog!"

"Oh, there are many like her," said Vassili, carelessly.

"Are there?" said Serejka, imitating him. "Ah, you peasants, you're all alike. As long as you gather your honey, it's all one to you."

"What's she to you?" broke in Vassili with irritation. "Have you come to ask her hand in marriage?"

"I know she's yours," said Serejka. "Have I ever bothered you? But now Iakov, your son, is all the time dancing around her, it's different. Beat him, do you hear? If not, I will. You've got a strong fist if you are a fool."

Vassili did not reply, but watched the boat as it turned about and made toward the beach again.

"You are right," he said finally. "Iakov will hear from me."

"I don't like him. He smells too much of the village," said Serejka.

In the distance, on the sea, was opening out the pink fan formed by the rays of the rising sun. The glowing orb was already emerging from the water. Amid the noise of the waves was heard from the boat the distant cry:

"Draw in!"

"Come, boys!" cried Serejka, to the other fishermen on the beach. "Let's pull together."

"When you see Iakov tell him to come here to-morrow," said Vassili.

The boat grounded on the beach and the fishermen, jumping out, pulled their end of the net so that the two groups gradually met, the cork floats bobbing up and down on the water forming a perfect semi-circle.

* * * * *

Very late on the evening of the same day, when the fishermen had finished their dinner, Malva, tired and thoughtful, had seated herself on an old boat turned upside down and was watching the sea, already screened in twilight. In the distance a fire was burning, and Malva knew that Vassili had lighted it. Solitary and as if lost in the darkening shadows, the flame leaped high at times and then fell back as if broken. And Malva felt a certain sadness as she watched that red dot abandoned in the desert of ocean, and palpitating feebly among the indefatigable and incomprehensible murmur of the waves.

"What are you doing there?" asked Serejka's voice behind her.

"What's that to you?" she replied dryly, without stirring.

He lighted a cigarette, was silent a moment and then said in a friendly tone:

"What a funny woman you are! First you run away from everybody, and then you throw yourself round everyone's neck."

"Not round yours," said Malva, carelessly.

"Not mine, perhaps, but round Iakov's."

"It makes you envious."

"Hum! do you want me to speak frankly?"

"Speak."

"Have yon broken off with Vassili?"

"I don't know," she replied, after a silence. "I am vexed with him."

"Why?"

"He beat me."

"Really? And you let him?"

Serejka could not understand it. He tried to catch a glimpse of Malva's face, and made an ironical grimace.

"I need not have let him beat me," she said. "I did not want to defend myself."

"So you love the old grey cat as much as that?" grinned Serejka, puffing out a cloud of smoke. "I thought better of you than that."

"I love none of you," she said, again indifferent and wafting the smoke away with her hand.

"But if you don't love him, why did you let him beat you?"

"Do you suppose I know? Leave me alone."

"It's funny," said Serejka, shaking his head.

Both remained silent.

Night was falling. The shadows came down from the slow-moving clouds to the seas beneath. The waves murmured.

Vassili's fire had gone out on the distant headland, but Malva continued to gaze in that direction.

* * * * *

The father and son were seated in the cabin facing each other, and drinking brandy which the youth had brought with him to conciliate the old man and so as not to be weary in his company.

Serejka had told Iakov that his father was angry with him on account of Malva, and that he had threatened to beat Malva until she was half dead. He also said that was the reason she resisted Iakov's advances.

This story had excited Iakov's resentment against his father. He now looked upon him as an obstacle in his road that he could neither remove nor get around.

But feeling himself of equal strength as his adversary, Iakov regarded his father boldly, with a look that meant: "Touch me if you dare!"

They had both drunk two glasses without exchanging a word, except a few commonplace remarks about the fisheries. Alone amidst the deserted waters each nursed his hatred, and both knew that this hate would soon burst forth into flame.

"How's Serejka?" at last Vassili blurted out.

"Drunk as usual," replied Iakov, pouring our some more brandy for his father.

"He'll end badly—and if you don't take care you'll do the same."

"I shall never become like him," replied Iakov, surlily.

"No?" said Vassili, frowning. "I know what I'm talking about. How long are you here already? Two months. You must soon think of going back. How much money have you saved?"

"In so little time I've not been able to save any," replied Iakov.

"Then you don't want to stay here any longer, my lad, go back to the village."

Iakov smiled.

"Why these grimaces?" cried Vassili threateningly, and impatient at his son's coolness. "Your father's advising you and you mock him. You're in too much of a hurry to play the independent. You want to be put in the traces again."

Iakov poured out some more brandy and drank it. These coarse reproaches offended him, but he mastered himself, not wanting to arouse his father's anger.

Seeing that his son had drunk again, alone, without filling his glass, made Vassili more angry than ever.

"Your father says to you, 'Go home,' and you laugh at him. Very well, I'll speak differently. You'll get your pay Saturday and trot—home to the village—do you understand?"

"I won't go," said Iakov, firmly.

"What!" cried Vassili, and leaning his two hands on the edge of the table he rose to his feet. "Have I spoken, yes or no? You dog, barking at your father! Do you forget that I can do what I please with you?"

His mouth trembled with passion, his face was convulsed, and two swollen veins stood out on his temples.

"I forget nothing," said Iakov, in a low tone and not looking at his father. "And you—have you forgotten nothing?"

"It's not your place to preach to me. I'll break every bone in your body."

Iakov avoided the hand that his father raised over his head and a feeling of savage hatred arose in him. He said, between his clenched teeth:

"Don't touch me. We're not in the village now."

"Be silent. I'm your father everywhere."

They stood facing each other, Vassili, his eyes bloodshot, his neck outstretched, his fists clenched, panted his brandy-smelling breath in his son's face. Iakov stepped back. He was watching his father's movements, ready to ward off blows, peaceful outwardly, but steaming with perspiration. Between them was the table.

"Perhaps I won't give you a good beating?" cried Vassili hoarsely, and bending his back like a cat about to make a spring.

"Here we are equal," said Iakov, watching him warily. "You are a fisherman, I too. Why do you attack me like this? Do you think I do not understand? You began."

Vassili howled with passion, and raised his arm to strike so rapidly that Iakov had no time to avoid it. The blow fell on his head. He staggered and ground his teeth in his father's face.

"Wait!" cried the latter, clenching his fists and again threatening him.

They were now at close quarters, and their feet were entangled in the empty sacks and cordage on the floor. Iakov, protecting himself as best he could against his father's blows, pale and bathed in perspiration, his teeth clenched, his eyes brilliant as a wolf's, slowly retreated, and as his father charged upon him, gesticulating with ferocity and blind with rage, like a wild boar, he turned and ran out of the cabin, down towards the sea.

Vassili started in pursuit, his head bent, his arms extended, but his foot caught in some rope, and he fell all his length on the sand. He tried to rise, but the fall had taken all the fight out of him and he sank back on the beach, shaking his fist at Iakov, who remained grinning at a safe distance. He shouted:

"Be cursed! I curse you forever!"

Bitterness came into Vassili's soul as he realized his own position. He sighed heavily. His head bent low as if an immense weight had crushed him. For an abandoned woman he had deserted his wife, with whom he had lived faithfully for fifteen years, and the Lord had punished him by this rebellion of his son. His son had mocked him and trampled on his heart. Yes, he was punished for the past. He made the sign of the cross and remained seated, blinking his eyes to free them from the tears that were blinding them.

And the sun went down into the sea, and the crimson twilight faded away in the sky. A warm wind caressed the face of the weeping peasant. Deep in his resolutions of repentance he stayed there until he fell asleep shortly before dawn.

* * * * *

The day following the quarrel, Iakov went off with a party to fish thirty miles out at sea. He returned alone five days later for provisions. It was midday when he arrived, and everyone was resting after dinner. It was unbearably hot. The sand burned his feet and the shells and fish bones pricked them. As Iakov carefully picked his way along the beach he regretted he had no boots on. He did not want to return to the bark as he was in a hurry to eat and to see Malva. Many a time had he thought of her during the long lonely hours on the sea. He wondered if she and his father had seen each other again and what they had said. Perhaps the old man had beaten her.

The deserted fisheries were slumbering, as if overcome by the heat. In the inspector's office a child was crying. From behind a heap of barrels came the sound of voices.

Iakov turned his steps in that direction. He thought he recognised Malva's voice, but when he arrived at the barrels he recoiled a step and stopped.

In the shade, lying on his back, with his arms under his head, was Serejka. Near him were, on one side, Vassili and, on the other, Malva.

Iakov thought to himself: "Why is father here. Has he left his post so as to be nearer Malva and to watch her? Should he go up to them or not."

"So, you've decided!" said Serejka to Vassili. "It's goodbye to us all? Well, go your way and scratch the soil."

A thrill went through Iakov and he made a joyous grimace.

"Yes, I'm going;" said Vassili.

Then Iakov advanced boldly.

"Good-day, all!"

The father gave him a rapid glance and then turned away his eyes. Malva did not stir. Serejka moved his leg and raising his voice said:

"Here's our dearly beloved son, Iakov, back from a distant shore."

Then he added in his ordinary voice:

"You should flay him alive and make drums with his skin."

Malva laughed.

"It's hot," said Iakov, sitting beside them.

"I've been waiting for you since this morning, Iakov. The inspector told me you were coming."

The young man thought his voice seemed weaker than usual and his face seemed changed. He asked Serejka for a cigarette.

"I have no tobacco for an imbecile like you," replied the latter, without stirring.

"I'm going back home, Iakov," said Vassili, gravely digging into the sand with his fingers.

"Why," asked the son, innocently.

"Never mind why, shall you stay?"

"Yes. I'll remain. What should we both do at home?"

"Very well. I have nothing to say. Do as you please. You are no longer a child. Only remember that I shall not get about long. I shall live, perhaps, but I do not know how long I shall work. I have lost the habit of the soil. Remember, too, that your mother is there."

Evidently it was difficult for him to talk. The words stuck between his teeth. He stroked his beard and his hand trembled.

Malva eyed him. Serejka had half closed one eye and with the other watched Iakov. Iakov was jubilant, but afraid of betraying himself; he was silent and lowered his head.

"Don't forget your mother, Iakov. Remember, you are all she has."

"I know," said Iakov, shrugging his shoulders.

"It is well if you know," said the father, with a look of distrust. "I only warn you not to forget it."

Vassili sighed deeply. For a few minutes all were silent.

Then Malva said:

"The work bell will soon ring."

"I'm going," said Vassili, rising.

And all rose.

"Goodbye, Serejka. If you happen to be on the Volga, maybe you'll drop in to see me."

"I'll not fail," said Serejka.

"Goodbye."

"Goodbye, dear friend."

"Goodbye, Malva," said Vassili, not raising his eyes.

She slowly wiped her lips with her sleeve, threw her two white arms round his neck and kissed him three times on the lips and cheeks.

He was overcome with emotion and uttered some indistinct words. Iakov lowered his head, dissimulating a smile. Serejka was impassible, and he even yawned a little, at the same time gazing at the sky.

"You'll find it hot walking," he said.

"No matter. Goodbye, you too, Iakov."

"Goodbye!"

They stood facing each other, not knowing what to do. The sad word "goodbye" aroused in Iakov a feeling of tenderness for his father, but he did not know how to express it. Should he embrace his father as Malva had done or shake his hand like Serejka? And Vassili felt hurt at this hesitation, which was visible in his son's attitude.

"Remember your mother," said Vassili, finally.

"Yes, yes," replied Iakov, cordially. "Don't worry. I know."

"That's all. Be happy. God protect you. Don't think badly of me. The kettle, Serejka, is buried in the sand near the bow of the green boat."

"What does he want with the kettle?" asked Iakov.

"He has taken my place yonder on the headland," explained Vassili.

Iakov looked enviously at Serejka, then at Malva.

"Farewell, all! I'm going."

Vassili waved his hand to them and moved away. Malva followed him.

"I'll accompany you a bit of the road."

Serejka sat down on the ground and seized the leg of Iakov, who was preparing to accompany Malva.

"Stop! where are you going?"

"Let me alone," said Iakov, making a forward movement. But Serejka had seized his other leg.

"Sit down by my side."

"Why? What new folly is this?"

"It is not folly. Sit down."

Iakov obeyed, grinding his teeth.

"What do you want?"

"Wait. Be silent, and I'll think, and then I'll talk."

He began staring at Iakov, who gave way.

Malva and Vassili walked for a few minutes in silence. Malva's eyes shone strangely. Vassili was gloomy and preoccupied. Their feet sank in the sand and they advanced slowly.

"Vassili!"

"What?"

He turned and looked at her.

"I made you quarrel with Iakov on purpose. You might both have lived here without quarrelling," she said in a calm tone.

There was not a shade of repentance in her words.

"Why did you do that?" asked Vassili, after a silence.

"I do not know—for nothing."

She shrugged her shoulders and smiled.

"What you have done was noble!" he said, with irritation.

She was silent.

"You will ruin my boy, ruin him entirely. You do not fear God, you have no shame! What are you going to do?"

"What should I do?" she said.

There was a ring of anguish, or vexation, in her voice.

"What you ought to do!" cried Vassili, seized suddenly with a fierce rage.

He felt a passionate desire to strike her, to knock her down and bury her in the sand, to kick her in the face, in the breast. He clenched his fists and looked back.

Yonder, near the barrels, he saw Iakov and Serejka. Their faces were turned in his direction.

"Get away with you! I could crush you!"

He stopped and hissed insults in her face. His eyes were bloodshot, his beard trembled and his hands seemed to advance involuntarily towards Malva's hair, which emerged from beneath her shawl.

She fixed her green eyes on him.

"You deserve killing," he said. "Wait, some one will break your head yet."

She smiled, still silent. Then she sighed deeply and said:

"That's enough! now farewell!"

And suddenly turning on her heels she left him and came back.

Vassili shouted after her and shook his fists. Malva, as she walked, took pains to place each foot in the deep impressions of Vassili's feet, and when she succeeded she carefully effaced the traces. Thus she continued on until she came to the barrels where Serejka greeted her with this question:

"Well, have you seen the last of him?"

She gave an affirmative sign, and sat down beside him. Iakov looked at her and smiled, gently moving his lips as if he were saying things that he alone heard.

"When will you go to the headland?" she asked Serejka, indicating the sea with a movement of her head.

"This evening."

"I will go with you."

"Bravo, that suits me."

"And I, too—I'll go," cried Iakov.

"Who invited you?" asked Serejka, screwing up his eyes.

The sound of a cracked bell called the men to work.

"She will invite me," said Iakov.

He looked defiantly at Malva.

"I? what need have I of you?" she replied, surprised.

"Let us he frank, Iakov," said Serejka. "If you annoy her, I'll beat you to a jelly. And if you as much as touch her with a finger, I'll kill you like a fly. I am a simple man."

His face, all his person, his knotty and muscular arms proved eloquently that killing a man would be a very simple thing for him.

Iakov recoiled a step and said, in a choking voice:

"Wait! That is for Malva to—"

"Keep quiet, that's all. You are not the dog that will eat the lamb. If you get the bones you may be thankful."

Iakov looked at Malva. Her green eyes laughed in a humiliating way at him and she fondled Serejka so that Iakov felt himself grow hot and cold.

Then they went away side by side and both burst out laughing. Iakov dug his foot deep in the sand and remained glued to the spot, his body stretched forward, his face red, his heart beating wildly.

In the distance, on the dead waves of sand, was a small dark human figure moving slowly away; on his right beamed the sun and the powerful sea, and on the left, to the horizon, there was sand, nothing but sand, uniform, deserted,—gloomy. Iakov watched the receding figure of the lonely man and blinked his eyes, filled with tears—tears of humiliation and painful uncertainty.

On the fishing grounds everyone was busy at work. Iakov heard Malva's sonorous voice ask, angrily:

"Who has taken my knife?"

The waves murmured, the sun shone and the sea laughed.

Milton Keynes UK
Ingram Content Group UK Ltd.
UKHW030912151124
451262UK00006B/789